SYRACUSE UNIVERSITY 12600557

SO-BFE-004

3 2911 00784362 6

DATE DUE

14 Jul '64 CAS   30 JAN '67 S S

12 Nov '64 G M   1 1

17 NOV '65 CG

JUL 66 D N

1 DEC '66 MK

JAN   APR 1 1 1987

MAY 0 5 1987   BIRD

CLASS AND NATIONALITY

CLASS and NATIONALITY

English and American Studies

Joel B. Montague, Jr.

Professor of Sociology
Washington State University

COLLEGE AND UNIVERSITY PRESS ● New Haven, Conn.

IN ASSOCIATION WITH

WASHINGTON STATE UNIVERSITY
Pullman, Washington

Copyright © 1963 by College and University Press Services, Inc.

Library of Congress Catalog Card Number 62-19468

MANUFACTURED IN THE UNITED STATES OF AMERICA BY
UNITED PRINTING SERVICES, INC.
NEW HAVEN, CONN.

ACKNOWLEDGMENTS

We wish to acknowledge, with thanks, the granting of permissions to quote passages pertinent to this monograph from the works of others. Material from *Max Weber, An Intellectual Portrait*, by Reinhard Bendix (copyright 1960 by Reinhard Bendix) is reprinted by permission of Doubleday and Company, Inc. Quotations from *The English Middle Classes*, by Roy Lewis and Angus Maude, are printed by permission of Alfred A. Knopf, Inc. T. H. Marshall has given permission to use a quotation from *Citizenship and Social Class*. Permission to use material from *Nationalism and After* has been granted by the author, E. H. Carr, St. Martin's Press, Inc., New York, and by Macmillan and Company, Ltd., London. Oxford University Press, London, has given permission to quote from *Sociology*, by Morris Ginsberg. The *British Journal of Sociology* and Routledge and Kegan Paul, Ltd., publishers, have granted the use of a quotation from "The Conception of the Middle Classes," by G. D. H. Cole, and the same publisher has given permission to quote from *Studies in Class Structure* by G. D. H. Cole. The Free Press, Inc. has given permission to use material from *Social Mobility in Britain*, edited by D. V. Glass. Permission to quote from *Report of the Central Advisory Council for Education—England*, "15 to 18," Volume I (Report), has been granted by the Controller of Her Britannic Majesty's Stationery Office. *The Sociological Review* and Melvin Tumin have given permission to reprint material from "Some Principles of Stratification: A Critical Analysis." Eyre and Spottiswoode, Ltd., London, and William Morrow and Company have given generous permission to quote from *Life in Britain*, by J. D. Scott.

CONTENTS

LIST OF TABLES

INTRODUCTION*

Sociology is concerned with both people and societies, with personal problems and public issues; in C. Wright Mills's terms, with both biography and history. This dualistic interest is obligatory because the two cannot, in reality, be separated. The major problem of all social science is to determine, in all its complexity, the nature of the relationship between the individual and society. Some kind of balance must be kept between these two aspects of sociology.

In contemporary sociology in the United States, it frequently appears that inordinate attention is given to problems of individuals in society. Attitudes are elicited, behavior is observed and recorded, and individual deviation is measured; but this is only half the task. Such work tells us what people are like and how they behave. Sociology is also obliged to address itself to finding out what *society* is like and how it changes or can be

---

* This monograph has grown out of a series of studies which began at the London School of Economics and Political Science during the academic year, 1950-51. The data which are utilized in the cross-cultural studies included in this book were collected by a research group of which I was a member at that time. The American data were collected in Spokane and Seattle, Washington. Additional work was done in the English Midlands in 1957 and 1962. My English associates are, of course, in no way accountable for the analysis and interpretation in these papers. The English essays may reveal the naïve and myopic view of the "outsider" as well as whatever objectivity may be gained by partial blindness. The research work and publication were supported, in part, by the Committee on Research, Washington State University. Permission to use previously published material has been given by: *The American Sociological Review; The British Journal of Sociology; Social Forces; Sociology and Social Research; The Pacific Sociological Review; Rural Sociology;* and *Research Studies*, Washington State University. Continued association—intermittent though it has been—with A. H. Halsey (Oxford University), has been most helpful. The assistance of Bernard Phillips and Edgar Epps, former Research Assistants at WSU, is gladly acknowledged, and the constant helpfulness of my wife, Evelyn (University of Idaho) is sincerely appreciated.

changed. Sociology has been defined by some as the study of the origin, structure, and development of societies—which of course includes individuals—but also makes social stratification, nationality, and social movements as pertinent as delinquency, personality, and prostitution.

There are many reasons, both historical and methodological, for the seeming emphasis upon the personal behavior side of sociology. Admittedly, considering the present state of our methodology and conceptualization, it is difficult to study empirically the big problems—the society-wide problems.

Class and nationality, however, have taken on increasing significance in modern times. The development of the nation-state, supported by those particularly strong in-group sentiments, ideas, and practices which we call nationalism, has been perhaps the most important social influence in the modern world. In this process of historical-cultural development, the concept of national sovereignty was solidified and the nation became the center of the cultural life of most individuals and groups.

Concomitant with the rise of nationalism has been the differentiation of national populations into classes. In this process, western capitalistic nations have developed somewhat similar systems of stratification. Without being concerned about definitions at this point, it is clear enough that following the commercial and industrial revolutions, the middle classes came into prominence and power through the ownership of property and control of business organizations. At the same time the urban masses working for wages multiplied and took on the characteristics of a proletariat.

Some students thought that the class way of life—the class culture—would in time supersede the influence of the nation-state. Marx thought, even in his day, that "The proletarian is without property; his relation to his wife and children has no longer anything in common with the bourgeois family-relations; modern industrial labor, modern subjection to capital, the same in England as in France, in America as in Germany, *has stripped him of every trace of national character.*"[1]

It is true that in all modern industrial nations the working classes have developed along somewhat similar lines, as have the propertied classes, each class deriving a distinctive economic orientation and style of life which tends to cut across the boundaries of the nation-state. Even so, nationality is still a fundamental differentiating factor. These similar class arrangements are the product not only of what the nations have had in common in industrial capitalism, but they also reflect the unique historical-cultural growth of each nation-state.

Some social scientists have addressed themselves to the problem of assessing the influence of class and/or nationality upon personality. The "national character school"—for example, Mead, Bateson and Gorer—all recognize status or social class differences in a society. They tend to see them as "versions of" and "systematically related to" the wider cultural pattern. Linton has developed the concept of "status personality" and he gives considerably more weight to class influence upon personality than do most of his colleagues. He says ". . . the members of each class are shaped by their own culture and their personality norms derive first of all from this culture and only secondarily from the culture of the larger configuration of which their class forms a part."[2]

It may be that the national character students have assumed a larger degree of homogeneity in national culture than can be justified.[3] Nations do have their own unique historical-cultural experience. As Lerner has said ". . . it remains true that nations are realities, that their cultures develop along different lines and in different ways, and that the world inside the heads of their people is a characteristic world."[4]

The United States and England, of course, share much of the western European religious-political-economic heritage. They share a common language; they are both nominally Christian countries having a representative form of government; they subscribe to similar conceptions of civil liberties, individual freedom, and equality before the law; they both share in large part the same literature and modes of artistic expression. But the institutionalization of these ways of life has proceeded differently in each country. Nevertheless, England and the United States are both class societies. Their respective systems of stratification have, however, developed in relation to quite different historical situations and it may be assumed that the two status systems as they are related to the larger societies are not only different from each other, but that they are conceptualized in somewhat different fashions by the respective populations.

In order to study the relationship between class and nationality, or indeed to analyze either separately, it is necessary to have some reasonably clear definition of these phenomena. Through the process of abstraction they must be conceptualized. The present status of *class, nationality,* and *national character* as concepts in sociology is confused.

The central concept of social class has been subject to several interpretations and has been emphasized in a variety of ways. Marx, Max Weber, Parsons, and Warner have each contributed generously to the contemporary state of confusion. Or, it may be more sanguine to say that each of these messiahs speaks with clarity but their disciples have interpreted their messages badly. The concept of nationality has been pre-empted by the political scientists, and national character is the stepchild of anthropology. Although both concepts are appropriate tools for sociological analysis, neither has been consistently or widely employed. With no eschatological pretention, these concepts are examined in Part I of this monograph with a view to better understanding.

Part II consists of two essays which may illustrate the analytical use of the concepts of class, status, and power as well as provide an abbreviated "over-view" of contemporary English and American social structure.

In Part III the social class structure of England is seen in somewhat more detail through a series of important segments of English society. The working class, the middle class, professionals, small farmers and other occupational groups are viewed against the backdrop of the welfare state. Socialized medicine and contemporary education are also discussed. These studies illustrate the relation between class and status in a changing society.

A series of comparative studies based upon samples of English and American boys comprises Part IV. These studies illustrate the use of the concepts class and nationality, with some implications for national character. The hypothesis of a high degree of cultural homogeneity overriding class and the subcultures of geographical regions is questioned.

Robert Lynd, some years ago, called for the formulation of "outrageous hypotheses." He warned that if we do not question the existing social structure, much of our work will in effect be a rationalization of it. We will find ourselves largely concerned with trying to make whatever exists "work better." This is a danger of functionalism. Sociology, as all science, must be concerned with innovation. Class and nationality exist in the modern world. Our task is not only to find out "what they are like," and "how they work," but to call them into question—to form outrageous hypotheses, i.e., "nationality is obsolete in the modern world"; or "national identity is not dependent upon national sovereignty"; "classes are dysfunctional in a democratic society"; or "increased class consciousness in terms of rational self-interest will facilitate the democratic process and avoid the threat of mass society."

It hardly need be said that the following studies, although within the scope of these hypotheses, are not addressed to testing them. It is hoped that they may bring about somewhat more interest in an understanding of what have been called the big sociological problems of our time.

PART ONE

THE CONCEPTS:
Class, Nationality, National Character

chapter one

SOCIAL CLASS

Observable differences in social position are present in all societies. At the level of folk knowledge, no doubt, people have always recognized invidious distinctions. The man who had the best cave and the most bearskins seemed also to have privileges and social position not shared by the Neanderthal masses. The ownership of property, whether it be bearskins, copper gongs, cattle, land, machines or money, clearly made a difference. Social position, style of life, influence, and power frequently could be seen to be associated with property ownership. The propertyless, on the other hand, found themselves in less enviable positions.

Even at this level of analysis, however, it was perfectly clear that other attributes than the ownership of property resulted in differential social position. Indeed, property in the material sense may be owned in common and thereby no one could receive special advantage. Nevertheless distinctions seem to arise. Those who were the "first comers," the "early settlers," the "first families" received some special honor, or those having an unusual talent, special knowledge, or mystical power received respect and deference from the rest. At the level of folk knowledge it sometimes seemed impossible to determine why some people had higher social standing than others—it had always been so. The men had more privileges than the women; the old men more than the young men. The draper had more than the cobbler and the butcher more than the fishmonger.

Sociologists have considered the phenomenon of social stratification as one deserving considerable attention. To raise the analysis above the folk level it was necessary to define the problems and proceed within the frame of reference of scientific study. Broad descriptive categories were formed, such as classes, estates, and castes. Ideal types were formulated, such as "the estate society," "the adaptive society," "the open class society," etc. Concepts and theory were developed as a basis for research and as a result of research. Concepts are abstractions which are the result of perceptions of the real world. Well-defined concepts are the tools of research and analysis.

In contemporary sociology considerable confusion has arisen in regard to the definition and proper use of existing concepts. The term *class* is often confused with *status* or *status group*. The correlates of class and status are likewise unclear. The relationship between class and social honor, prestige, influence, power, and party has not been clearly established. There is a basic disagreement as to whether classes are functional or dysfunctional in society; whether they form a continuum or can be defined as discrete groupings; whether classes are society-wide phenomena or limited to the community; whether they are objective or subjective categories—real or imaginary—and there is the question as to whether classes are essentially conservative or radical in regard to social change.

With a view to understanding where this diversity of concepts and theory came from rather than with the thought of eliminating it, the contributions—to both confusion and clarification—of certain sociologists of the past century and the present will be examined briefly.

Karl Marx

Karl Marx was not primarily a sociologist but rather should probably be classified as a classical economist. He did, however, contribute significantly to sociology, and many sociologists have spent much time and effort refuting, revising, or reaffirming his work or certain pertinent parts of it. Certainly in the area of social stratification Marx can no more be ignored than can Freud in psychology or Darwin in biology. One might say that just as Freud tried to develop a theory of the evolution of the self, and Darwin developed a theory of biological evolution, Marx's intention was to provide a scientific account of the evolution of society and social change. As a sociologist Marx was interested in: (1) the economic structure of society; (2) the ideological superstructure; (3) social revolution; and (4) the future of society.[5] Marx's emphasis upon the economic structure of society was not new; it was a very common approach of historians and economists of his time. Marx's contribution, in this sphere, was the context in which he discussed the economic structure. He was concerned with the historical development of human labor as the primary relation between men and nature. Also, in his attempt to classify human societies in terms of their economic systems he went beyond others of his time.

The concept of ideological superstructure was a more original contribution. As Marx developed and used the concept it became almost synonymous with non-material culture, including ideas, law, morals, politics, religion, art, philosophy. Marx's effort was of course to analyze the relation of this cultural superstructure to what he called the "real basis" of society, that is, the mode of production. He attempted, then, to establish correlations between certain stages of economic and technological development and what amounted to the rest of culture—including the class structure.*

The third area of sociological interest was his analysis of social change and particularly of revolution, and the fourth theme of his sociological work was concerned with the nature of society in the future. Marx was critical of the utopians. He thought of his work as "scientific socialism" which was at the same time a body of scientific knowledge and an incentive to political action.

Although it is well known that Marx made the concept of class central to his conception of both history and revolution, it is difficult to pinpoint his ideas from his writings. Marx's writings, it should be kept in mind, represented a wide variety as to purpose, content, and style. They consisted of political debates, speeches, manifestos, calls to action on the one hand, and theoretical heavily documented tomes on economics on the other. Class may be seen as a factor in the dialectical—almost automatic

---

* This economic or technological determinism was somewhat modified according to Engels, as is mentioned later.

—working out of historical change, or it may be used in a call to action against immediate employers.

Marx started chapter fifty-two of Volume III of *Capital* with the heading "The Classes." Unfortunately he wrote only a page and a half, stopped, and never finished it. Several scholars have taken the responsibility for finishing this chapter for Marx. Dahrendorf, although he warns ". . . the claim that I have written the unwritten last chapter of *Capital* must not be understood literally in the sense of a philological conjecture," has probably done the best work in collating the material in an imaginative fashion.[6] There are of course in addition to the original works, many commentaries on Marx's and Engels' writings that are related to sociology and more specifically to social class.[7] There is no attempt made in the present writing to give either a complete or sufficient critique of Marx on social class. Certain pertinent generalizations and interpretations are presented.

Marx, at various times and places, spoke of a number of classes. At the beginning of the famous unfinished chapter on social classes he enumerated "wage labourers," "capitalists" and "landowners" as ". . . the three great classes of modern society based on the capitalist mode of production."[8] In other places Marx referred to the "middle class," the "bourgeoisie," the "petty bourgeoisie," the "social scum" *(lumpenproletariat)*, "the aristocracy," etc. The most common Marxist construction was of course a two-class society, the bourgeoisie and the proletariat; the property owners and the propertyless; the employer and the wage worker; the exploiter and the exploited. The same dichotomy was used in describing pre-capitalistic societies in the beginning of the *Communist Manifesto*: "Freeman and slave, patrician and plebeian, lord and serf, guildmaster and journeyman, in a word, oppressor and oppressed. . . ."[9]

Engels, in a note included in the 1888 English edition of the *Manifesto*, defined the bourgeoisie and the proletariat as follows: "By bourgeoisie is meant the class of modern capitalists, owners of the means of social production and employers of wage-labour. By proletariat, the class of modern wage-labourers who, having no means of production of their own, are reduced to selling their

labour-power in order to live."[10] The two-class system was a sim-
plification, but it was a heuristic device which emphasized the
heart of the matter. It is easier to have two opposed classes than
to have three or four. These were the major classes of capitalist
society; they stood diametrically opposed; they waited only for
widespread class consciousness to initiate overt conflict. The other
classes would be forced to align themselves with one or the
other of these clearly differentiated groups.

Marx frequently used two phrases which were basic not only
to the formation of the two classes but to his entire system—the
"mode of production" and the "relations of production." In general
terms, mode of production referred to the particular way in
which the factors of production—land, labor, capital, and entre-
preneurial function—were arranged for the production of goods.
Slavery, the manorial system, handicraft, and the factory system
in modern capitalism represented, in broad outline, modes of
production. The relations of production referred to the typical
authority relationships—and other human relations—associated
with a particular mode of production. In slavery, this would mean
the relations between owner and worker. The slave had no free-
down, no rights, was forced to work, may have owned his own
tools, was provided food and housing and protection—was exploited as property. The wage worker was free—sometimes free to
starve—owned no tools, had no security in food or housing, and
was dependent upon the sale of his labor for a livelihood.

Social class according to Marx depended in the first instance
upon one's relation to the mode of production. This created the
class situation. All persons finding themselves in the same class
situation, Marx thought, would develop a similar style of life and
similar attitudes and values about many things. Thus the two
classes would be set apart. Marx maintained that the gap
between the life situations of worker and capitalist was not
sufficient for the formation of a class. Class is dependent upon
the development of antagonism between the two groups—dependent upon a community of feeling which arises from widespread class consciousness.

This second element in class formation is a result of the relations of production. It is through the impact of the authority

relations, working conditions, levels of wages and the like that class consciousness arises among the workers and becomes the cementing factor which forms all people who find themselves in the same class situation into a social class. Marx further maintained that the authority relations in production determined authority relations in the society. This moved the whole problem into the political area. Every class struggle thus became a political struggle.[11]

Political parties represented class interests and provided the mechanism through which class conflict could be carried on. The party is merely the politically organized class.*

This short consideration of Marx in relation to existing concepts of social class is not concerned with Marxism as an ideological system or social philosophy. Without discussing dialectical materialism as a theory of history, something can be said about the general idea of economic determinism. From the brief discussion above it is clear that economic factors in the mode of production and the relations of production, in property ownership and wage labor, are the basic determinants of social class. Class struggle, through purposeful social action or through the working out of the dialectical process, changes the course of history.

It should be pointed out, however, that Marx and Engels were possibly not quite as particularistic—not quite as narrowly economically deterministic as they have sometimes been portrayed. A few quotations, although admittedly out of context, may throw some light on this problem:

> . . . According to the materialist conception of history, the *ultimately* determining element in history is the production and reproduction of real life. More than this neither Marx nor I have ever asserted. Hence if somebody twists this into saying that the economic element is the only determining one, he transforms that proposition into a meaningless, abstract, senseless phrase. The economic situation is the basis, but various elements of the

---

* This concept of party is used as a rationalization for a one-party system in countries which have experienced a victorious Communist revolution—there being no privately owned industry, no propertied class—only one party is needed to represent the workers.

superstructure—political, juristic, philosophical theories, religious views and their further development into systems of dogmas, also exercise their influence upon the course of the historical struggles and in many cases preponderate in determining their form. . . . Thus there are innumerable intersecting forces, an infinite series of parallelograms of forces which give rise to one resultant—the historical event. . . . Without making oneself ridiculous it would be a difficult thing to explain in terms of economics the existence of every small state in Germany, past and present. . . .

. . . Marx and I are ourselves partly to blame for the fact that the younger people sometimes lay more stress on the economic side than is due to it. We had to emphasize the main principle *vis-a-vis* our adversaries who denied it, and we had not always the time, the place nor the opportunity to allow the other elements involved in the interaction to come into their rights.[12]

Marx's concept of class may be not quite as purely economic as it is sometimes portrayed to be. Certainly it has an objective economic base in relation to the mode of production, but the origin of class consciousness is in the relations of production and these relations are as social as they are economic. Class consciousness is itself a psychological phenomenon, and when Marx's classes go into action, so to speak, they take the form of political parties. Thus Marx included in one rubric, *class* (objective economic position), *subjective identification* and the element of *power*. These classes were society-wide potential social movements which could modify (or support) the societal status quo.[13]

Max Weber

Weber, like Marx, was concerned with the study of whole societies, and with the relationships and influences existing among major social institutions. Weber saw society as a balance between opposing forces. Whereas Marx thought that he had shown the dominating influence of economic institutions in society, much of Weber's work was an attempt to demonstrate the influence of religious and other institutions upon economic arrangements.

Three main themes were explored by Weber in a massive lifelong research: (1) the effect of religious ideas on economic

activities; (2) the relation between social stratification and
religious ideas; and (3) the delineation of the distinguishing
characteristics of western civilization.[14]

Weber assumed that society was a composite of positively
or negatively privileged status groups competing with each other.
Status groups had their own economic interests, status honor, and
general orientation toward the world. Each group tried to preserve or enhance its position by means of social distance, exclu-
siveness, and by monopolizing economic opportunities. He used
this concept of society in his studies of the landed aristocracy,
the rising bourgeoisie, the bureaucracy, and the working class
in imperial Germany. He used the same perspective in his study
of the great religions of the world. Weber made intensive researches of the religious leaders of ancient China, India, and
Palestine. Each group of religious leaders was seen as a distinctive status group with a particular style of life. Weber tried to
analyze the social conditions under which the charismatic
inspirations of the religious leaders first became the style of life
of a small group of religious converts and then eventually the
dominant orientation of a whole civilization. "In each case
Weber attempted to trace a style of life to the particular group
or groups from which a characteristic pattern of conduct and
ideas had spread. In this way the culture of a nation can be
constructed as an outgrowth of group power and group conflict
in its historical development."[15]

These works, which became comparative studies in the broad
sense, cannot be explored here. Of course the study which is
best known is *The Protestant Ethic and the Spirit of Capitalism.*[16]

Bendix has set out in the form of propositions what he considers the salient points in Weber's approach to the study of
"social organization." With the listing of these the discussion will
have to proceed to Weber's conception of class, status, and party.

(1) Every society is divided into several social strata that are
characterized by the esteem in which they are held, by their monopolistic practices in social and economic life, by a specific style
of life and by a distinctive, more or less articulated world view.
(2) Collective actions—including economic actions—that are
based on ideal and material considerations of status run counter

to all collective actions that are based entirely on the cash-nexus. (3) As members of a status group, individuals are the product of a social organization. The actions and ideas of individuals may be studied, therefore, as attributes of that social organization.

(4) Status groups may be—and frequently are—the fountainhead of moral ideas that shape the conduct and world view of the individuals belonging to them, and that may affect the self-interested actions of a larger number of others. On the other hand, the ideas of the few may provide also the basis for the formation of a status group.

(5) Such ideas are in the first instance responses to the challenges of the material environment. . . . However, the world view of a status group is never solely a response to material conditions or a product of economic interest. It is also the product of ideas that are the result of human inspiration in response to a spiritual challenge. . . .[17]

Max Weber frequently conceived of society as being composed of three major orders: the economic, the social, and the legal or political. Each of these orders was made up of groupings and, as indicated above, these groups were seen as competing in many ways. This resulted in a balance between groups or in the gradual domination of one set of groups over the others. Either result brought a certain amount of stability to society.

Now in general terms the units of the economic order were *classes*; the units of the social order were *status groups*; and the units of the legal-political order were *parties*.

The term "class" refers to any group of people . . . [who have the same] typical chance for a supply of goods, external living conditions, and personal life experiences, insofar as this chance is determined by the . . . power . . . to dispose of goods or skills for the sake of income in a given economic order. . . . Class situation is, in this sense, ultimately "market situation."[18]

It is clear that the basis of class is economic—the unequal distribution of economic power and hence the unequal distribution of opportunity. In Weber's early studies of the *Junkers* and farm workers in Germany, however, he emphasized that the collective action of these groups could not be understood in economic terms alone. It was necessary to study each group as a subculture, to look into the "style of life" exhibited by the Junkers, their patriarchal manner, their sense of honor and prestige, their personal conceit and their "world view"; just as it was necessary to understand the pride of the farm workers and their resistance to personal subservience.

As Bendix points out, a concept had to be formulated that would encompass the influence of ideas upon the formation of groups without losing sight of economic conditions.[19] For this grouping, which was essentially a unit of the social order, Weber used the term *stand* which is interpreted as "status group." Weber says,

> In contrast to the economically determined "class situation" we wish to designate as "*status situation*" every typical component of the fate of men that is determined by a specific, positive or negative, social estimation of *honor*. . . . In content, status honor is normally expressed by the fact that a special *style of life* can be expected from all those who wish to belong to the circle. Linked with this expectation are restrictions on "social" intercourse (that is intercourse which is not subservient to economic purposes) these restrictions may confine normal marriages within the status circle. . . .
>
> Stratification by status goes hand in hand with a monopolization of ideal and material goods or opportunities. . . . Besides the specific status honor, which always rests upon distance and exclusiveness we find all sorts of material monopolies. Such honorific preferences may consist of the privilege of wearing special costumes, of eating special dishes, taboo to others, of carrying arms. . . . Status groups are the specific bearers of all "conventions."[20]

It should be pointed out that although there are economic elements in the status situation, the two concepts "class" and "status group" are antithetical in many kinds of collective action. Economic transactions—the market—recognizes no social or honorific distinction. The market is, as Weber said, "oriented toward a rationally motivated adjustment of interest."[21] In the status order, on the other hand, economic factors are outweighed by prestige, honor, and tradition. All actions of status groups are oriented to the "feeling of the actors that they belong together."[22] Thus wealth may not be considered as a valid basis of prestige and status. If wealth were the criterion of status, then the *nouveau riche* might have more prestige than the not-so-rich old families. This would undermine the status system. The communication and interaction within a status group is such that it forms a community in Weber's terms. Whatever conflict exists within or between status groups is for the achieving of, or maintaining of, positive privilege whereas *class struggle* is, in a sense, impersonal and is oriented to economic ends. Weber agrees with Marx as to the historical relevance of class struggle, and in the next sentence is critical of Marx's "false class consciousness."

> That men in the same class situation regularly react in mass actions to such tangible situations as economic ones in the direction of these interests that are most adequate to their average number is an important and after all simple fact for the understanding of historical events. . . . However, this fact must not lead to that kind of pseudo-scientific operation with the concept of "class interests" so frequently found these days, and which has found its most classic expression in a statement of a talented author, that the individual may be in error concerning his interests but the "class" is infallible about its interests.[23]

In a short statement, which he says may be an "over-simplication," Weber reveals again both his alignment with and divergence from Marx: ". . . one might . . . say that 'classes' are stratified according to their relations to the production and acquisition of goods; whereas 'status groups' are stratified according to principles of their *consumption* of goods as represented by special 'styles of life.' "[24]

Parties, the units of the legal-political order, "live in a house of power."[25] Whereas Marx saw classes as ultimately becoming power groups—political parties—Weber thought that parties could be formed from either classes or status groups and added that ". . . they need be neither purely 'class' nor purely 'status' parties. In most cases they are partly class parties and partly status parties, but sometimes they are neither."[26] Parties may be either short-lived or long-enduring and may attain power by various means, "from naked violence of any sort to canvassing for votes. . . . Their aim is not necessarily the establishment of a new . . . territorial dominion. In the main they aim to influence the existing dominion."[27]

Max Weber must be given credit for differentiating between class, status group, and party to what would seem to be an obvious advantage in empirical research and analysis. One cannot inquire into the relations between these important factors in social stratification unless they are first conceptually separated.[28]

Talcott Parsons

Parsons, a contemporary sociologist, along with Kingsley Davis and Wilbert E. Moore is a leading exponent of functionalist theory in social stratification. Functionalism-nonfunctionalism is one of the great debates in present-day sociology. This very brief discussion, however, cannot enter into the broader problems involved. It is not concerned with the general theory of functionalism in its various interpretations, revisions, and extensions. In the area of social stratification, however, it is apparent that functional analysis frequently tends to portray classes in a class society as being necessary to the integration and on-going of that society, as are castes in a caste society and estates in a feudal society. It is postulated that each society has a basic, common value system. Through the concept of "social action," which refers to any goal-oriented behavior in relation to the basic values, individuals make choices—evaluations—which result in differential ranking as to status. Thus Parsons defines stratification as "the ranking of units in a social system in accordance with the standards of the common value system."[29] Thus stratification is seen as an inescapable consequence of social interaction.

The evaluations, Parsons says, are made in reference to "qualities," "performances," and "possessions." Qualities presumably refer to ascribed traits such as intelligence or noble birth; performances refer to behavior, such as role or occupation; and possessions are thought to include not only material possessions but also special talent, skill, or knowledge. The social evaluation of these attributes as to whether they are high or low, desirable or undesirable, is dependent upon the nature of the existing basic value system of the particular society.

Parsons' theoretical system provides concepts and categories which have heuristic value in research and descriptive analysis.

It says little or nothing about the phenomena of social class in the real world, which was the major object of attention of Marx and Weber.

Kingsley Davis and Wilbert Moore

The functionalist debate in social stratification centers on Davis and Moore rather than on Parsons. This may be because Parsons' work is clearly—or not so clearly—at a high level of abstraction, whereas it appeared that Davis and Moore's formulations were not so far removed from social reality, although in answer to criticism they say that their "theory" also represented a high degree of abstraction.

The discussion started in 1945 with the publication of Davis and Moore's paper "Some Principles of Stratification." Although Davis may have thought that he terminated the argument by making functionalism "synonymous with sociological analysis" in his presidential address in Chicago, 1959, others are not convinced. So the debate goes on.[30]

In the original 1945 paper "Some Principles of Stratification,"[31] Davis and Moore assume that no society is "classless or unstratified" and they try to "explain, in functional terms, the universal necessity which calls forth stratification in any social system."[32] At the very beginning they point out that they are discussing a system of differentiated positions, not the individuals which occupy them. However, this becomes somewhat confused as the discussion proceeds.

The "functional necessity" arises out of the fact that all societies must somehow distribute their members in social positions and must activate them to perform the duties of these positions. Some positions are "inherently more agreeable than others," and some are "functionally more important than others. . . . Inevitably, then, a society must have, first, some kind of rewards that it can use as inducements and second, some way of distributing these rewards differentially according to positions. The rewards and their distribution become a part of the social order, and thus give rise to stratification."[33] Davis and Moore conceive of several kinds of rewards: "Things that contribute to sustenance and comfort," "things that contribute to humor and diversion," and "things that contribute to self-respect and ego expansion." These rewards, "rights," and perquisites vary with the position in relation to the social evaluation of functional importance which is presumably based upon some basic set of societal values and in relation to the differential scarcity of qualified personnel. They continue:

> If the rights and perquisites of different positions in a society must be unequal, then the society must be stratified, because that is precisely what stratification means. Social inequality is thus an unconsciously evolved device by which societies insure that the most important positions are conscientiously filled by the most qualified persons. Hence every society . . . must therefore possess a certain amount of institutionalized inequality.[34]

Although Davis later denies that he was "justifying" social inequality, he proceeds to show, using the M.D. as an example, that education and training is expensive and is obtained at some sacrifice. They conclude that: "This means . . . that the position must be high in the social scale—must command great prestige, high salary, ample leisure and the like."[35]

The remainder of the paper was devoted to a discussion of religion, government, wealth, property, labor, and technical knowledge as "major societal functions," and to some comment upon variation in forms of stratification with a warning against "trying to classify whole societies under such rubrics as caste, feudal, or open class."

Tumin, in 1953,[36] took upon himself the task of writing a "critical analysis" of the Davis-Moore theory of stratification. Davis maintained that Tumin was intent on eliminating social inequality rather than contributing to an explanation of it, but many, including the present writer, are of the opinion that Tumin did a necessary and on the whole, appropriate analysis.

Tumin first brings into question the basic assumption that social inequality is unavoidable and necessary in society. He asks how one decides which functions are more important than others. In a functionalist frame of reference "All acts and functions must be judged positively functional in that they constitute essential portions of the status quo." In the long run, for example, "*some* labor force of unskilled workmen is as important and as indispensable to the factory as *some* labor force of engineers."

As to the scarcity of talents which can be trained to fill the functionally more important positions in society, Tumin points out that in most societies no one knows how much talent exists in the population and that a smoothly working system of stratification would tend to keep anyone from finding out. The more rigidly stratified a society is, the less chance does that society have of discovering any new facts about the talents of its members.[37] For example, in a society where education is dependent upon the wealth of one's parents, a large part of the population may never have a chance to discover what "talents" it has.

The important fact about differential rewards and opportunities is whether or not they are socially inherited. If they are passed on to the next generation in such a system, then stratification is dysfunctional. Elites tend to restrict entrance into their privileged positions. The medical profession in the United States would be an example of this. If so, then it would be difficult to discover, recruit, and train persons for these "functionally more important positions." One could conclude, then, that a stratification system tends to reduce the survival chances of a society. Tumin says,

> It is only when there is genuinely equal access to recruitment and training for all potentially talented persons that differential rewards can conceivably be justified as functional. And stratification systems are apparently *inherently antagonistic* to the development of such full equality of opportunity.[38]

Davis and Moore maintained that the training period necessary to convert talents into skills was expensive and that sacrifice would have to be made by those requiring long training. First, Tumin observes that this sounds very much like the rationalization frequently offered by the more fortunate members of a society for their occupancy of privileged positions. Secondly, he points out that the training period of higher education cannot be considered a sacrifice in any sense—financially, psychically, or socially. And thirdly, the cost of such training could be assumed by the state. In this case there would be no need to compensate anyone in terms of differential rewards.

Tumin also argues that Davis and Moore have not fully explored the variety of motivations and rewards. He suggests that "joy of work," "instinct of workmanship," "work satisfaction," "social duty," and "social service," should be explored. "They have stated the case much too strongly when they insist that a 'functionally important position,' . . . 'must command great prestige, high salary, ample leisure, and the like' if appropriate talents are to be attracted to the position."[39]

Rewards may be so structured and so defined by the culture that it may not be *unavoidable* that differential prestige and esteem shall accrue to positions which command differential rewards in power and property.

Tumin concludes this "critical analysis":

> If the objections which have heretofore been raised are taken as reasonable, then it may be stated that the only items which any society *must* distribute unequally are the power and property necessary for the performance of different tasks. If such differential power and property are viewed by all as commensurate with the differential responsibilities, and if they are culturally defined as *resources* and not as rewards, then no differentials in prestige and esteem need follow . . . no known facts in psychological or social science have yet demonstrated [the impossibility or the] dysfunctionality for the continuity of a society [of developing] the tradition that each man is as socially worthy as all other men so long as he performs his appropriate tasks conscientiously.[40]

After thus disposing, at least to his satisfaction, of the Davis and Moore theory of the necessity and functionality of social stratification, Tumin makes the following "provisional assertions" as to the negative functions or dysfunctions of institutionalized social inequality in the form of a stratification system.

(1) Social stratification systems function to limit the possibility of discovery of the full range of talent available in a society. This results from the fact of unequal access to appropriate motivation, channels of recruitment and centers of training .

(2) In foreshortening the range of available talent, social stratification systems function to set limits upon the possibility of expanding the productive resources of the society, at least relative to what might be the case under conditions of greater equality of opportunity.

(3) Social stratification systems function to provide the elite with the political power necessary to procure acceptance and dominance of an ideology which rationalizes the *status quo*, whatever it may be, as "logical," "natural" and "morally right." In this manner, social stratification systems function as essentially conservative influences in the societies in which they are found.

(4) Social stratification systems function to distribute favorable self-images unequally throughout a population. To the extent that such favorable self-images are requisite to the development of the creative potential inherent in men, to that extent stratification systems function to limit the development of this creative potential.

(5) To the extent that inequalities in social rewards cannot be made fully acceptable to the less privileged in a society, social stratification systems function to encourage hostility, suspicion and distrust among the various segments of a society and thus to limit the possibilities of extensive social integration.

(6) To the extent that the sense of significant membership in a society depends on one's place on the prestige ladder of the society, social stratification systems function to distribute unequally the sense of significant membership in the population.

(7) To the extent that loyalty to a society depends on a sense of significant membership in the society, social stratification systems function to distribute loyalty unequally in the population.

(8) To the extent that participation and apathy depend upon the sense of significant membership in the society, social stratification systems function to distribute the motivation to participate unequally in a population.[41]

In 1958, Walter Buckley's article appeared in the *American Sociological Review*.[42] Buckley said that he was more concerned with the "methodological deficiencies" of the Davis-Moore theory than with its substantive content. He maintained in this well-argued paper, that Davis and Moore and the functionalists generally had confused *social stratification* with *social differentiation*. "To put the issue simply, . . . the current functional theory of stratification is not a theory of stratification at all, but something that more closely resembles a theory of certain

aspects of social differentiation and hierarchical organization."[43]
Davis and Moore, he maintains, disclaimed any interest in the
problem of stratification per se by claiming to concern themselves only with the "system of positions" of a society. Buckley
argues that "The term 'social strata' refers to social groups or
collectivities and not to positions, and that stratification refers
to the existence of strata in a society. . . ."[44]

The functionalists' theory fits in with the democratic ideology
—a person's social position should depend upon his own qualities
and achievements. Buckley says:

> The manner in which the functionalists present the stratifica-
> tion system as actually operating is rather the way in which
> many persons desire and believe that it would work in con-
> temporary society if only the class structure did not exist to
> hinder it! . . . Thus, it is precisely the issue of equality or in-
> equality of initial opportunity to acquire the qualifications
> socially defined as necessary for achievement of functionally
> important positions that is conspicuously absent from functiona-
> lists' theory.[45]

It appears that Buckley agrees with most of Tumin's criticism
of Davis and Moore, and in addition maintains that the functionalists have confused the process of differentiation—which
everyone would admit is universal and necessary—with social
stratification and reiterates the belief that the functionalists
ignore the social inheritance of status and class positions.[46]

Students with some historical orientation should find little
difficulty in supporting the view that stratification has been, on
balance, an actual or potential disruptive force.[47] Buckley maintains that social differentiation per se is not disintegrative. Differentiation and specialization of labor occur in all societies to
some degree. It is only with the next step, the social evaluation of
the differentiated roles, that invidious distinctions arise—that
is, in the process of social stratification. C. C. North, accepting
Durkheim's view, holds that increasing division of labor leads to
organic solidarity of cohesive interdependence, but also notes
that overspecialization and individualistically oriented interest
groups (classes?) are potentially disruptive.[48]

As to the "survival value" of stratification systems, it is just as reasonable to believe that certain societies have survived in spite of a caste system, or a class system, as it is to believe that such stratification systems were necessary for survival. Certainly stratification contributes to strains and stresses which make for instability as frequently as the converse is true.[49]

In the functional analysis of stratification systems there is the danger of undue emphasis upon the status quo. The assumption of equilibrium derived from early organismic theory, even when qualified in terms of "moving equilibrium," seems to be present, and one could conclude from such analyses that the existing distribution of negative and positive privilege should not be disturbed.

The problem is, however, not strictly one of functionalist-nonfunctionalist analysis. Lipset and Smelser have recently summarized the "division" in contemporary sociology showing that although contention continues over functionalist assumptions, it is largely a difference in "point of view" or frame of reference from which students approach problems of analysis. Some may see "the analysis of the consequences of specific historical situations [as] a more important 'explanation' of the 'system' than is the effort to specify the interrelated functions which the system and its parts serve at any given time." Or, on another level more closely related to the way "functional" has been used here, they say that the ". . . controversy [is] between the exponents of a functionalist and equilibrium concept of society and those who prefer to view society in dialectical terms as ever-changing and in a state of permanent conflict." They continue, "Sociology, it is maintained, because of its preoccupation with formal theory and precise methods, has moved away from the significant social and political problems, from the analysis of social change, the nature of power, and the extent of conflict and exploitation which exists in class systems. Many important problems are ignored because they do not fit a 'static' functionalist approach or because they cannot be measured precisely. . . . [These] critics maintain that functionalism becomes an endorsement of the *status quo.* . . ."[50]

Lipset and Smelser point out that the division or dichotomizing of approaches to the study of society is erroneous. They consider themselves to be historical and comparative oriented functionalists and quote Radcliffe Brown ". . . The two kinds of explanation do not conflict but supplement one another."[51] The efficacy of such a position is nearly beyond question; nevertheless, in stratification, as in other areas, somewhat divergent approaches have and do exist. Lloyd Warner, next to be considered, leaned toward the functionalist side.[52]

W. Lloyd Warner

Warner and Lunt published the first volume of the Yankee City Series in 1941.[53] The book was the result of a lengthy study by a large group of research workers. (Thirty are listed.) Warner is an anthropologist—a social anthropologist, and he describes his associates as social anthropologists.

Shortly before beginning the study of Yankee City (Newburyport, Massachusetts), Warner had completed a three-year study of the Stone Age people of Australia. He says, "The techniques I had used there to understand the social organization and mental life of the Australian blacks were those of social anthropology . . . my objective in studying them was not simply to understand how they organized their own social relations, but also to obtain a better understanding of how men in all groups, regardless of place or time, solve the problems which confront them. . . . My fundamental purpose in studying primitive man was to get to know modern man better. . . ."[54]

Awareness of this training and experience—and propensity for generalizing—is helpful in understanding Warner's work. The object of the study was to "describe in detail the cultural life of the community, emphasizing particularly the way in which these people have been divided into superior and inferior classes."

After two preliminary surveys had been made, they obtained an introduction to "one prominent man." He in turn introduced leaders of the research group to other important people in the community. Other introductions were arranged "which shortly spread our sources of information from top to bottom of the city" (population about 17,000). Although other sources of information were used, most of the data were obtained through interviews. Huge quantities of data were accumulated and analyzed.

The general frame of reference was a functionalist one. Warner saw the community as a complex of individuals, associations, and institutions interacting with each other—an "objective unity," a "fundamental or integrative" structure, a "working whole in which each part had definite functions." "It must be admitted that the analogy of the organism was in our thinking when we looked at the total community of Yankee City. . . ."[55]

The concept of class was not included in his discussion of the "conceptual framework," although the study had been described as being particularly concerned with class divisions. Later, however, Warner states that the original hypotheses about class "were subsumed under a general economic interpretation of human behavior. . . . It was believed that the fundamental structure of our society, that which ultimately controls and dominates the thinking and actions of our people is economic. . . ."[56] This economic, almost Marxian concept of class, however, was abandoned in the light of the data collected. Warner says that in the interviews some people mentioned that "money is not everything." Some wealthy persons seemed not to have the highest status. The converse was also true. Thus, social class was "discovered" in the community and was conceptualized, or better, defined as ". . . two or more orders of people who are believed to be, and are accordingly ranked by the members of the community, in socially superior and inferior positions."[57]

Two devices were used in the discovery of social class: The Index of Status Characteristics and Evaluated Participation. The first, consisting of four factors—occupation, source of income, house type, and dwelling area—was used by interviewers. Evaluated participation was carried on by the analysts and involved six techniques, which are self-explanatory: (1) matched agreements (that is, agreement of "several informants" on the class position of other people); (2) symbolic placement (informants identify others by superior or inferior symbols); (3) status reputation; (4) by comparison; (5) simple assignment; (6) institutional membership.

Warner found a high correlation between the two techniques (ISC and EP).[58] By these methods six classes were found to exist in Yankee City—the well known upper upper, lower upper, upper middle, lower middle, upper lower, and lower lower.

In Jonesville[59] Warner "found" only five classes, or rather, he combined the lower middle and the upper lower to form the "Common Man Level." Here again, he asserts that "these social levels are not categories invented by the social scientists to help explain what they have to say; they are groups recognized by the people of the community. . . ."[60]

In the introductory chapter of this book Warner maintains that Jonesville represents all other towns and cities: "The Jonesvilles, Smithtowns, Greenfields, and all the other -villes, -towns, and -fields of America are essentially alike . . . Dallas, Seattle, . . . Buffalo, . . . Atlanta, Springfield, or Walla Walla . . . no matter how the alphabetical letters are arranged they all spell Jonesville . . . Jonesville is in all Americans and all Americans are in Jonesville. . . . This is true for the urbanite office dweller . . . the devout acolyte . . . in a monastery, and the six generations of Jonesville. . . ."[61]

Warner and his associates had considerable influence on sociology, particularly the areas of social stratification and community studies, through the 1940's and 1950's. His work has received much attention and has been criticized severely.[62] The criticism pertains to theory, assumptions, concept of class, method and techniques employed, manner of analysis, and extent of generalization. We are primarily concerned with his concept of social class. However, as an illustration of dubious method and reporting, Lipset and Bendix have pointed out that in *Democracy in Jonesville* Warner used only ten informants. Nine of these were from the upper middle class. The informants, according to *verbatim* reports, used technical sociological terms such as "area in transition," "ecological and social strata," "cliques within the larger stratum," "social structure in outline," etc. One of the informants, a high school girl, analyzed the class structure of the whole town and presented a picture which agreed perfectly with Warner's even to the subdivisions of classes and the differences in family organization between classes. ". . . many of the panel members talk as if they were paraphras-

ing articles and books written by Warner."[63] Two possible explanations are suggested: the panel members were in such close
contact with members of the research team for such a long time
—from one to two years—that they began to see the town through
Warner's eyes, or the ten informants, nine being upper middle
class, were unusually conscious of class position and exceptionally
articulate on the subject.

Warner's method is, of course, related to his concept of class.
Indeed, he had no concept of class—other than a general economic orientation which was abandoned—until after class was
"discovered" through emphasizing his method and the analysis
of the data was being made. His work, in a sense, is a huge
survey. His method is essentially observation, classification, and
generalization.[64] Survey method and functional analysis may be
ahistorical[65] and, as Mills points out, can be carried on without
much knowledge of or pertinence to existing theory.

Regarding social class, Warner clearly puts his faith in "what
people think." Lipset and Bendix point out, however, that
". . . The analysis of any problem in the social sciences cannot
make people's opinion of that problem its point of departure."[66]
Mills refers to Warner's methods as ". . . ranking in terms of
status verbalization."[67] Class is what people—or some people—
say it is.

The study of public opinion and, for that matter, gossip, is a
legitimate pursuit for social scientists, but, if they are going to
do more than provide "more information about" something already known they must be concerned with aspects of these
problems of phenomena of which "people" are not aware.

Warner is criticized because he did not make use of existing
rather well-defined concepts in the area of social stratification.
Max Weber's delineation of concepts might have been useful.
Mills thinks so. He says:

> If Warner had availed himself of post-Marxian discussions in
> European sociological literature, and I refer especially to Max
> Weber, he would have "discovered" in a more exact form such
> things as he did "discover," as well as several more which would
> have enlarged his observational sensitivities, enabled him to ask

and perhaps to answer questions which he was not even able to raise within his own conceptual circle. If he had used an adequate apparatus, it would have ensured non-equivocation as to what he was talking about. . . .[68]

From these brief discussions of Marx, Weber, Davis and Moore, and Warner, one may gain some insight into the sources of the confusion which exists about the concept of social class. It may also be useful to dichotomize the varying views into objective and subjective approaches. The social scientists who emphasize the "economic aspects" of class, relation to the productive process, source of income, and occupation, fall into the objective category. These economic factors, when used as criteria of class, may be observed and measured with some degree of objectivity. Furthermore, the objectivists start with the observable, measurable phenomena and then try to determine what the relationship of these phenomena is to the individual and/or the society. The exponents of the objective view are most likely to be concerned with the power correlates of class and with social change. The subjectivists, on the other hand, do not ignore economic factors but are more concerned with the process of distribution and patterns of consumption. These, of course, are subject to some degree of objectification. The subjectivists, however, are apt to see class in terms of status, prestige, and reputation. Social class becomes a psychological phenomenon, a reputational level resulting from ascribed or achieved roles in the community. A particular "class" status may be obtained by the acquisition of status symbols which are defined by the community or society as having a certain honorific value. This concept of class may foster an interest in the status quo and in explaining tradition. "Classes" are not seen as potential conflict groups, or power groups, as the classes of the objectivists are apt to be considered, but rather as being more or less reciprocal in nature. Whatever "action" occurs is confined to striving within the existing system.

Part of the inconsistency and apparent confusion in the use of stratification concepts arises from the various value positions and ideologies held by different social scientists working in the field. Social scientists, as all scientists, hold some value orientation. These values, whatever they are and however derived, are inescapable. The denial of value judgments is itself a value position. Such value orientation may be made explicit, must be separated as far as possible from scientific procedures, but will very likely still influence the selection of problems and the choice of methodological tools—concepts. Lipset and Bendix have observed that "the ideological involvement of the social scientists who deal with social class, may be responsible for the methodological [and conceptual] confusion which prevails in this field."[69]

Social class is a part of social reality. Through perceiving this reality and the process of abstraction, the *concept* is formulated by social scientists and then becomes an epistemological tool in research. Studies such as Warner's tend to substitute people's awareness of class (status) for sociological concepts. At the theoretical level, it seems appropriate to consider *class, status,* and *power* as separable but interrelated concepts. The failure to do so results in "sponge concepts" which are of limited value in research and analysis. Obviously one cannot study the relations between these aspects of stratification unless they are first conceptually separated.

Warner, in abandoning the economic interpretation of class, and in ignoring the possibility of separating class, status, and power factors, in the end succeeded in confusing class with status, class with class-awareness, and class-awareness with status-awareness.

What Warner has done, in effect, is to form a status ladder of five or six easy steps up or down. This view is quite compatible with the basic myths of American society.

chapter two

NATIONALITY

Nationality is a condition of conscious group membership. The essence of nationality is the sharing of symbolic meanings, myths, memories, and values. This sharing is dependent upon adequate communication between the members of the community. Thus, one may be *of* the same community as others and *in* the same culture, but still not be a member of a community of people who have learned to communicate in such a way as to foster reciprocal understandings and appreciations of shared cultural elements. Nationality is not so much the result of the existence of such cultural elements as it is dependent upon the existence of sufficient communication between members of the community.

Deutsch has introduced the term "complementarity of communication"[70] by which he describes a high degree of complementary habits and facilities of communication. The test of complementarity of communication is its effectiveness. If effectiveness of communication is high in a community, the existing cultural elements form integrated and complementary patterns of communication, remembering, and acting. The people who experience these complementary patterns form, for the purposes at hand, a nationality.

The existence of a common language, place of residence, and the presence of common cultural elements is not sufficient to generate a feeling of nationality. It is the sharing process through adequate communication which brings about mutual understandings and appreciations leading to conscious membership in a nationality group. The sharing process does not necessarily require uniformity of language as is illustrated by the Swiss. "The Swiss may speak four different languages and still act as one people [nationality], for each of them has enough learned habits, preferences, symbols, memories, patterns of landholding and social stratification, events in history, and personal associations, all of which together permit him to communicate more effectively with other Swiss than with the speakers of his own language who belong to other peoples."[71] No magical congealing power is derived from speaking the same language. English-speaking peoples are, of course, members of various nationality groups, and are associated with distinct nation-states, as are Spanish-, German-, Dutch-, and French-speaking peoples. People residing in a particular nation-state and speaking the same language have commonly been considered as members of one nationality. This is not always true. If barriers to communication are of such significance as to prevent the development of a community of mutual understanding, peoples speaking basically the same language may not consider themselves members of the same nationality group. Examples of this situation would be the Scots and the Welsh. On the other hand, people residing in separate nation-states may consider themselves to be of one nationality. Znaniecki provides an example of this situation in the Polish-speaking people maintaining one nationality under three separate nation-states, and goes on to argue that nationality is not dependent upon a common political government, but it is the product of a specific social organization irreducable to political structures.[72]

Although nationality is not synonymous with language, homeland, or nation-state, and cannot be adequately defined in these terms, neither can they be ignored. Individuals who are the most conscious of nationality see in the national language the traditional bond of the community. Its use is considered the major means of educating the people in a common national consciousness. Language may be considered as a symbol of "national personality." Nationalism, which is apt to rise among the most keenly nationality-conscious, places great importance on the national language. "Nationalism . . . regards the absolute domination of the national language in its country as a matter of prestige and often claims the incorporation of all elements speaking the same language but living in other countries. . . . They, moreover, wish to purify their language from all foreign admixtures, they are jealous of every other language spoken in their country, and even resent it if foreigners speak their own tongue aloud in public."[73]

Homeland and a nation-state are, in the usual situation, of great significance for nationality. Many of the myths, symbols, memories, sentiments, and values which are common to a nationality have their origin in relation to the state. The idea of a certain territory as one's home and likely the home of his "fathers" gives rise to national sentiment and is an important element in nationality.

The nation-state and the concomitant concept of nationality are phenomena of modern times. Early in human history the family, through a simple division of labor, provided for all or most of man's basic needs. As human culture accumulated and became more complex, new groups, associations, and institutions arose in the process of increasing specialization and division of labor. The family became a clan, the clan a village. There was much specialization of labor in hunting and fishing societies and in pastoral economies. Village life, however, lent stability and continuity to social groups. It may be that in the primitive village all who lived within its bounds were not only in it but of it. A man identified himself by the village of which he was a member. He may have been, at the same time, a member of a family, a men's secret society, a group of religious functionaries, a member of a judicial council, but his widest affiliation providing a basis for adequate communication was with the village.

The Greek city-state represented the highest development of the village or town as an exclusive membership group. With the advanced culture of the Greeks, however, differentiation and specialization resulted in the demarcation of many special groupings within the city population. Highly specialized and complex political, economic, religious, military, educational, and artistic associations and institutions were present along with the ideologies and technologies necessary for the functioning of a small but intricate society. The feeling of belonging to a political unit was strong among only a portion of the inhabitants. Allegiance to the city was not shared by a large part of the people who lived within its walls. The slaves, freedmen, and residents of foreign origin had no interest in political affairs and felt no allegiance to the city. They, in fact, were neither expected nor allowed to evidence such an interest.[74] These prescribed classes were not subject to military service, although all citizens (except the poor, who could not afford to equip themselves) were compelled to serve in the army. The duties of military service and the risks of war were thus expected only of citizens—owners of property and proprietors of businesses—citizens who participated in affairs of the city and who felt a part of it.

There seems to have been relatively little consciousness of all Greek-speaking people as composing one nation or one nationality. Certain interrelationships between the city-states did exist in relation to non-Greeks. The Olympic Games and the Oracle of Delphi were common to all Greeks, but the barbarians were excluded from participation in these institutions. The city was the widest area of effective communication and political affiliation. This is illustrated by the fact that wars between the city-states were not thought of as civil wars.

During the Middle Ages men identified themselves with estates—peasantry, nobility, or clergy—and through a voluntary allegiance, to a prince. The Church was the one superordinated, "international" institution which claimed the primary allegiance of all. People speaking the same language felt no special unity and were frequently at war among themselves. It is true that the princes and kings evidenced a wider consciousness of language groups and political boundaries than did the masses of the people. Henri IV of France (1553-1610) is quoted as saying, upon receiving deputies of the newly acquired provinces of La Bresse and Pays de Gers: "As you speak the French language by nature, it is reasonable that you should be the subjects of a king of France. I quite agree that the Spanish language should belong to the Spaniard and the German to the German, but the whole region of the French language must be mine."[75] However, such statements are atypical even of the rulers. A prince or king desiring to expand his domain paid little attention to the language of the people he wished to subjugate.

The common people took little interest in the wars of their rulers unless they were bound by oath to military service, and then they fought for the prince, not for a community or nation. Voltaire could write in the eighteenth century: "That the princes are all the time maintaining so many soldiers, is really a deplorable disaster. But . . . this disaster produces something desirable: the people take no interest in the wars of their masters."[76]

As Sulzbach has pointed out, some of the great battles of the Middle Ages, which are frequently thought of as national, were in reality not national in character. For example, he cites the battle of Legnano (1176) in which the Lombard League defeated Emperor Frederick Barbarossa. It was a "local affair" in which Italians fought on both sides.[77]

Historians have pointed to many writers, particularly of the later Middle Ages, who had a sense of nationality, the feeling of nationalism, or the idea of national character. Rousseau, Herder, the Jacobins, Bentham, Mazzini, Maurras, Fichte, Hegel, Ranke, and Bismarck, among others, are included. These men were the forerunners of national consciousness. It should be kept in mind that they were all intellectuals, political leaders, and writers. There is no reason to believe that they reflected a consciousness among the masses of the people. Communication of all kinds was limited during this period. Even after the unification of the major European states, large segments of the population had no well-defined feeling of belonging to a national community. Medieval society was obviously not conducive to the development of nationality. In the traditional feudal society each estate recognized certain reciprocal obligations, but each estate lived in the manner to which it was accustomed and there was more homogeneity of estates than of nations. There was little basis for the sharing of common values between estates. Over and above the well-defined limits of one's estate Christianity provided a vague but powerful unity, but nationality is not the product of religious consensus. The Protestant Reformation, as it became identified with national leaders, helped to break down the one world of Christendom. The secular changes which accompanied the Industrial Revolution proved more effective in fostering national consciousness which is the basis for nationality. "Before the nineteenth century, it appears that the people at large were indifferent to what we call the 'principle of nationality.' Everything happened as if they experienced no national consciousness."[78]

In the first centuries after the Middle Ages, the word "nation" was used in Germany and France for designating the higher ruling classes in opposition to the *volk* or people, which correspond to the English words "populace" or "common people." The word nation and the idea of nationality became associated with power and sovereignty. The ruling classes were frequently called "the nation."[79] The German historian Archenholtz wrote in 1793: "By a nation I understand the upper classes of the people only."[80] The French writer, J. Fievée, at the beginning of the nineteenth century elaborated the same idea.

> Rousseau made a mistake and misled all minds with a single word, the word "people." Whenever you meet in the *Contrat Social* the word "people," replace it by the word "nation," and you will be greatly surprised to find that what impressed you before has lost its sense. The reason is simple. I am not saying that in France and almost all countries of the world, "people" represents the idea of that part of the nation which by its poverty and lack of education is naturally excluded from the discussion of great interests of the State. I am going much further . . . the French people is not equivalent to the French nation. The nation implies the citizens, the Government, the laws, and even the habits, which in the word "people" in its widest sense, the Government may not be comprised, which leads to all errors of the *Contrat Social*.[81]

These views were more in keeping with the times than were those of Rousseau. It was only in the ruling classes that that consciousness of national myths and memories existed. It was largely within the ruling class that they were transmitted. Complementarity of communication was confined by class barriers. The common people had but little sense of nationality. Nevertheless it may be held that it was with Rousseau that the modern concept of nationality and the accompanying idea of nationalism emerged. Rousseau rejected the idea that the nation could be identified with the ruling class. It appeared that in his writings he made nation and people synonymous, and thereby formulated a principle which was operative in both the French and American revolutions. Rousseau, however, was thinking in terms of the "Third Estate"—the relatively new middle classes—rather than in terms of the whole people. This represented a broadening of the concepts of nation and nationality, but was not a departure from the previous identification of nation with political power. The ruling middle classes were now the bearers of nationalism.

These shifts in power relations and the extension of nationalism were the results of increased communication through which the middle classes were not only able to identify themselves with the national myths, memories, and values, but to become a part of them, supported by the political and economic philosophy of individualism and laissez faire. The rights of property became identified with the rights of man. Property was the basis of full membership in the nation. An owner of property has "a stake in the country."[82] Economic interest and class identification were the bases of conscious recognition of nationality. Individually it meant national political rights and collectively it was the basis of both economic and political rights of nations in international affairs.

The propertyless working class was thus effectively denied a similar feeling of belonging. Marx's appeal to the working classes of all countries to unite was a recognition of this relative lack of national identification of the working class. From this point of view the workers had no fatherland. Full recognition of national membership of the working class was dependent upon further industrialization and the accompanying organization which led to increased communication among the working class and between it and the propertied classes. The increasing strength of the trade-union movement, expanded educational opportunities, and heightened political interest and participation, laid the groundwork for the kind of communication basic to nationality.

Carr emphasizes essentially these factors in what he refers to as "the climax of nationalism" and discusses their effect on national policy.

> The rise of new social strata [the working class] to full membership of the nation marked the last three decades of the 19th Century throughout western and central Europe. Its landmarks

were the development of industry and industrial skills; the rapid
expansion in numbers and importance of urban population; the
growth of workers' organizations and the political consciousness
of the workers; the introduction of universal compulsory education; and the extension of the franchise. These changes, while
they seemed logical steps in a process inaugurated long before,
quickly began to affect the content of national policy in a revolutionary way. . . . The primary aim of national policy was no
longer merely to maintain order and conduct what was narrowly
defined as public business, but to minister to the welfare of
members of the nation and to enable them to earn their living.[83]

This transition from the "night watchman" state to the "welfare
state" and the change in national policy which it implies, brought
the masses into full membership in the nation and into conscious
recognition that their welfare was tied to the national welfare.
Although this process has gone further in England and has
bridged a larger gap between classes there than in the United
States, the same processes, delayed somewhat in time, have
been at work here. Socialization thus has its natural corollary
in the nationalization of socialism, fostering what Carr refers
to as the twentieth-century alliance between nationalism and
socialism.[84]

Inclusive nationality would then seem to be dependent upon
the existence of democratic process and socialization. However,
totalitarian states may generate a high degree of national feeling
with the absence of democratic process and with a minimum
of socialization. This was the case in Germany under Hitler
where National Socialism was more national than social. The
degree of complementarity of communication necessary for sharing national myth, memories, and values may result from authoritarian manipulation and indoctrination as well as from actual
participation in the political process. Modern mass communication lends itself equally well to propaganda and to education.
As Deutsch pointed out, the complementarity of communication
is measured by the effectiveness of the technological system,
not by the nature of the message transmitted.[85]

At the present time in Asia and Africa many countries are confronted with the problem of organizing the state in such a way as

to foster the rapid development of national consciousness. In such countries, lacking both mass education and a tradition of democratic process, totalitarianism may provide a more effective means of increasing complementarity of communication than do democratic arrangements and parliamentarianism. In countries which do not share the conceptions of human rights, individual liberties, and civic responsibilities common in the West, the existence of political parties and the slow and sometimes malfunctioning of the democratic process appear to be divisive rather than unifying.

Although national consciousness has been broadened by both authoritarianism and democratic processes, it would be a mistake to overestimate the level of consensus of nationality in the nations of the modern world. The USSR and the USA are, in a sense, both multi-nationality states as is, of course, the British Commonwealth. Class and caste still operate as barriers to communication and thereby to unity of nationality. Carr says that: "Today in the most nation-conscious of all epochs—it would still probably be fair to say that a large numerical majority of the population of the world feel no allegiance to any nation."[86]

The level of consciousness of nationality is not consistent within a national population. Whole classes who have had only the slightest awareness of nationality during times of peace, become conscious of their membership and responsibilities in war. The level of national feeling at any one time is proportional to the effectiveness of communication and its utilization for national purposes.

Both the concepts of nation and nationality are of recent origin in human history. The allegiance of primitive man was familial or tribal; the allegiance of the Greeks was to the city, and was limited to only a portion of the residents; the first allegiance of man in the Middle Ages was to the church and then to his estate. The wars of expansion and national unification were carried on by princes, monarchs, and the ruling classes and they were thought of as constituting the whole of the nation. The rise of the bourgeoisie broadened the consciousness of nationality after the Industrial Revolution, but it was only with the recognition of the working class and the new national policy of social and economic welfare for the masses that nationality came to include a large portion of the people of a nation-state.

The recognition and partial integration of the masses of the people in modern national societies were made possible by mass communication which was utilized for authoritarian indoctrination as well as for the extension of the democratic process.

The nation and consciousness of nationality are historical phenomena. They are neither universal in time nor space, both being characteristic of certain periods and certain parts of the world. Today nationalism is high in the west, has largely replaced internationalism in socialist countries, and is the major force behind revolutionary changes in the so-called underdeveloped countries. There are, however, the beginnings of regional organizations which differ somewhat from previous attempts to establish spheres of influence, power alliances, and the like. The difference is seen in the strong functional element in present regional organizations. Such beginnings may lead to a regionalism which will function as a transitional structure between the nation and nationality on the one hand and true internationalism and world citizenship on the other. There is considerable evidence, at the present time, that the nation is obsolete as a unit of both military and economic organization.[87] It will surely involve a long period of time, but with the wider recognition of this obsolescence of national organization, movement toward desegmentalization by nationality of the world's population may be evident.

chapter three

NATIONAL CHARACTER

In ancient times traders, travelers, and military men who had contact with cultural groups other than their own, made many observations on life in foreign countries. They reported that the people in other lands were different in many ways from the people of their homeland. Sometimes they attempted to explain these differences by reference to climate, race, "humours," or some other factor—real or mystical. Thus, long before the existence of modern nations and the wide recognition of nationality, the Egyptians, Greeks, Romans, and Byzantines—or rather certain individuals among them—believed that peoples of different nations had different personalities.

The stereotypes of "foreign peoples" thus developed were at the folk-knowledge level, based upon individual experience. They were unorganized, unscientific, and likely to be particularistic. They did not, for the most part, have reference to nations in the modern sense of the term.

Intuitive and particularistic theories and explanations of personality differences—national or otherwise—are still postulated and are accepted by many people. Today there are the racists, geographical determinists, endocrinologists, nutritionists, and mystics, each of whom can account for personality differences without the slightest deviation from his particular discipline. The area of investigation which has come to be known as national character study is so far removed from either the folk-knowledge of the ancients or the unilateral formulations of the particularists that only the slightest significance can be attached to either as predecessors of contemporary endeavor.

National character study, as it has developed in the last fifteen or twenty years, is usually considered to be a part of social anthropology. Most, if not all national character studies, however, are of such a nature as to involve other disciplines, particularly psychology and sociology. Although anthropologists, psychologists, and sociologists had given much attention to the study of personality in its many aspects long before World War II, it was during the war period that the present national character school began its major researches. Interest was focused upon other peoples in terms of *nationals* of allied or enemy countries. This accounts for the term "national" being used rather than "social character," or "basic character." It may also account for the rather rapid adaptation of anthropological theory and methods previously used in the study of small "primitive" societies to the study of large complex modern nations. These considerations, along with the applied orientation in connection with psychological warfare, may be responsible for the lack of consistent theory in the area of national character study.

At the present time national character, as applied to modern nations, should be kept in the realm of a theoretical concept—a hypothetical entity that may or may not exist. Linton makes a distinction between basic personality and national character. He holds that a basic personality type can be established by determining the personality elements which are held in common by members of a society, but he is not so certain about national character. "These common personality elements together form a fairly well-integrated configuration which may be called the *Basic Personality Type* for the society as a whole. The existence of this configuration provides the members of the society with common understandings and values. . . ."[88] However, he says, "The step from the concept of basic personality to that of national character is a long one and one which cannot be said to have been scientifically validated as yet."[89] Basic personality, for Linton, represents the norm, or the "common denominator" of elements which all members of a society share. He thinks it is a useful concept and that it can be established in small, relatively homogeneous societies.

Inkeles and Levinson in a critique of national character, consider it to be a hypothetical entity. "If modal personality structures cannot be found in modern nations then the term national character, at least as currently defined, will acquire the status of an empirically useless concept . . . we are now only in the process of determining whether national character constitutes a genuine field of study."[90]

Geoffrey Gorer and Margaret Mead give national character a somewhat more secure place in social anthropology. Gorer says that the basic hypotheses are ". . . exactly the same as those employed in the analysis of primitive national character (except that one has to expect regional or class differences) but the data on the basis of which the deductions are made are of a somewhat different, and on the whole, much less satisfactory nature."[91] He points out that "The test of the hypotheses about national character is the same as the test for any other scientific hypotheses; it is accurate prediction."[92]

Mead also sees national character studies as extensions of the general area of culture and personality. She states that the national character studies utilize the same premises and methods as are used in the personality and culture field, but that ". . . historically it has had two distinguishing features: the group of persons with a shared social tradition whose culture is studied is selected because they are the citizens or subjects—the nationals—of a sovereign political state, and the society *may* be so inaccessible . . . that less direct methods of research have to be used."[93]

The term national character is sometimes used to refer to certain aspects of a culture which give it a distinctive character or ethos. However, it is more commonly employed in reference to the personality of members of a national population. Thus, Gorer says: ". . . it is the study of personality in culture, people in their social setting . . ." and ". . . [it] is an attempt to isolate and describe the motives shared by the members of a society who manifest the same shared habits or cultures."[94] This is similar to the use of the term by Margaret Mead.[95] Linton considers national character to represent personality norms composed of ". . . cultural elements shared by the various social units which compose such a nation. . . . They reflect a common denominator of the personalities of the nation's members." Although as pointed out earlier, he is doubtful about the existence of such a character in reference to modern nations.[96]

Kardiner, using somewhat different terminology, stresses the element of compatibility of personality with the culture. Basic personality is conceived of by Kardiner as that personality structure which is most congenial to the prevailing institutions of the society. Fromm, using the term "social personality," stresses not the frequency of its occurrence but the element of *requiredness* by the society.[97]

Inkeles and Levinson discuss the positions of Linton, Kardiner, and Fromm and point out the implied distinction between the socially required or most congenial personality structures and the actual modal personality structure.[98]

The idea which runs through all of these definitions of national character, or basic personality structures, is that the individuals of a society embody a series of shared behavior patterns. This raises the question of the distribution of such shared patterns. The terms "mode," "norm," "standard" have been used to describe the presumed distribution. Most of the writers in the field conceive of national character as being unimodal in nature. Inkeles and Levinson agree that national character can, or should, be equated with modal personality. However they suggest that ". . . a multimodal conception of national character would seem to be theoretically the most meaningful as well as empirically the most realistic. . . ." They think that this is particularly true in reference to complex modern nations.[99]

The distribution of any set of behavior patterns or of any attitude-value system among the individuals in a national population is dependent upon the degree of complementarity of communication among the members of the society. Sharing can only take place through communication. Although consciousness of nationality is more widespread in the modern world than ever before, the existing state of urbanization, industrialization, and division of labor gives modern society a certain secondary and segmental nature. Consciousness of nationality has increased despite the formation of apparently more distinct economic classes. Class and other discontinuities in national character are discussed later.

As was mentioned earlier, national character studies have made use of psychology in both their general theoretical orientation and in the analysis of data. Psychoanalytic theory has been widely used. By psychoanalytic theory is meant some modification or revision of Freudian theory. Neo-Freudianism with an emphasis upon cultural dynamics appears to have the most utility in the analysis of data. Learning theory has been necessary in national character studies in relation to the socialization process. This is usually in the form of some kind of "conditioned-response" or "pleasure-pain" learning theory.[100]

There is no standardized method or analytical scheme in evidence in delineating modal personality or national character. A combination of techniques has been used. The major approaches which may be combined or used separately are: (1) a thorough analysis of the culture of a society; (2) a study of adult individuals by interviews, the use of projective tests, etc., and the life history; (3) a study of the experiences of early childhood, child training practices, and the whole socialization process.[101]

According to Gorer, the data gathered by the field worker can be divided into three categories: (1) the psychological functions of the institutions; (2) the emotional response of the adults; and (3) the experiences and vicissitudes of the children.[102] These approaches are based upon certain assumptions about the nature of culture and the psycho-physiological nature of the individual. Margaret Mead has delineated them in some detail.[103] In abbreviated form they are as follows: (1) the psychic unity of mankind; (2) individual differences due to genetic factors; (3) Cultures have systematic aspects which can be referred to the biologically given characteristics of their human characters, such as maturational sequences, hand-eye coordination, etc.; (4) Some systematic aspects of culture may be referred to other regularities in nature; (5) Cultures may be seen as historically patterned systems of communication giving meaning to certain symbolic behavior; (6) the wholistic nature of culture—causing change in one part to affect other parts; (7) the uniqueness of a culture resulting from a sequence of historical events; (8) A culture changes with the introduction of outside elements—natural or social. (Formulations based upon assumptions 3, 4, 5 and 6 cannot predict the occurrence of such changes, but can establish the limits of such changes); (9) Each member of a society contributes to the perpetuation and reinterpretation of cultural forms as they are passed on to the next generation. Changes in behavior of any individual will be noticed, but only changes in a category of members can be expected to result in changes in the whole system; (10) Cultures show comparable features when cross-cultural categories are applied to them in such a way that the unique pattern of organization of each culture is also taken into account; (11) Cultural subgroups manifest a "version of the wider cultural patterns;" (12) "Any member of a group, provided that his position within that group is properly specified, is a perfect sample of the group-wide pattern on which he is acting as an informant. . . . Two boys with very different social backgrounds—one being a deaf mute—are equally perfect examples of American national character, *provided that their individual position and individual character-istics are taken fully into account.*"[104] (13) "Any cultural state-ment must be made in such a way that the addition of another class of informants previously unrepresented will not change the nature of the statement *in a way which has not been allowed for in the original statement.* . . . (That is, the anthropologist samples in terms of the structure of the group he is studying, and he is responsible for building a sufficiently good model of that struc-ture to enable him to place each informant within it and describe accurately the deficiencies of his material)."[105]

There would seem to be but little disagreement with Mead on the assumptions dealing with the biological and psychological nature of man, the nature of culture, and the assumption that culture is transmitted to the next generation through learning.

Assumptions 12 and 13 may raise questions in the minds of most sociologists and some anthropologists. In national character studies dealing with modern societies, it seems doubtful that the anthropologist can build a sufficiently good model of the social structure to permit the use of one individual as an adequate sample of the society. If national character is to be thought of in terms of modal personality it is necessary to adhere as closely as possible to accepted ideas of sampling. This does not mean that studies of individuals and of groups, and studies using so-called "purposive" samples, cannot make significant contributions to the field of national character analysis. However, as Linton maintains, "To establish the actual personality norms for different societies it is necessary to submit a fair random sample of their members to individual study."[106] A random or other representative sample of the adult population of a modern nation has never been employed in the study of national character. Students most interested in the area would not deny the usefulness of such a sample, but they apparently feel that it is not necessary. Most of the studies have concentrated upon the behavior patterns of a relatively few adult individuals, upon the culture as expressed in institutions and collective documents such as motion pictures and books, or have been largely concerned with child training and the socialization process.

In the study of individual personality, projective tests and questionnaires, life-history documents, and both structured and unstructured interviews have been utilized. The use of semi-structured clinical interviews is illustrated by Dick's studies of Germans and Russians.[107] The major criticism of this approach is the limited scope of the data. Their value on the other hand is in the intensive nature of the studies.

Probably the most frequent approach to the study of modal personality or national character is represented in analyses of cultural phenomena. These studies have been concerned with the unique aspects of institutionalized patterns, particularly in the areas of political behavior, religious ideas and practices, content of mass media, etc. Through such study, major cultural themes may be identified. It is postulated that such basic cultural themes, values, and attitudes are internalized by all normal persons in the society, with exceptions made by some students for class and regional differences. A major technique following this approach is the interpretive study of collective documents. In this category of cultural phenomena folk tales and music may be included as well as books, popular stories, motion pictures, radio and television programs.

These studies have made a considerable contribution to knowledge in the field of national character analysis. The question which may be raised is in regard to a possible disparity between the data and the *real* culture—that is, the way most people actually think and behave. Such analyses may reveal what has been referred to as the *ideal* culture rather than the real culture. This is not to say that the ideal is of little significance in personality formation, but to point out that the real and ideal cannot be equated and that the statistical mode, if data were available for its computation, might well fall outside the range of the ideal.

Another technique employed in establishing basic themes, attitudes, and values in a society is illustrated by the recurring "plot." The plot is a psychocultural phenomenon which may be found re-enacted in many different social situations. This concept was used by Mead and Bateson in their study of Bali and by Gorer in his work with Japanese culture. It is not very different from Opler's concept of "themes."[108] In Balinese culture, a recurring plot identified the female as taking the initiative in erotic relationships and as acting the role of seducer of the responsive male, but she ceases her approaches at the last moment, leaving the male in a disturbed state. This plot or theme has been observed in child rearing and in common ceremonial dances. Here, again, the question arises as to the manner in which the majority of people in the society interpret the plot. Is it more closely related to the ideal culture than to the real behavior of human beings? Such a theme may be well known—universal in the society—and still have relatively little effect upon the actual, everyday behavior of people. The searching out of such plots and themes, however, may provide fruitful hypotheses concerning modal personality, or national character.

The third approach to the problem of identifying and studying national character places much emphasis upon child-rearing practices. This method pays particular attention to child-training techniques, as it is maintained that it is through these techniques that the major themes of the culture are passed on to the new members of a society. The child takes on the culture in a relatively few easy lessons and is thus prepared to meet a variety of social situations which are ordered in terms of the major themes which he has previously internalized.[109]

Some of these studies have given the impression that a specific childhood experience resulting from a particular training or care technique is directly linked with, or causal to, a specific adult personality trait. For example, Gorer and Rickman appear to take an ". . . inductive leap from the experience of swaddling in childhood to impassivity and controlled rage as adult traits in the 'Great Russians.' "[110] This is unfortunate, because Gorer denies making the assumption of such a direct causal relationship between a childhood experience and adult personality. It is not the technique which in itself is a causal factor, but rather the technique or a series of child-training techniques, which function as carriers of basic themes in the culture. It is through these experiences that the fundamental motives, meanings, and cultural expectations are acquired by the new members of the society.

Child-training studies must, therefore, be closely integrated with analyses of the culture and studies of individual adult personality. In the study of national character, basic cultural themes and adult character should not be inferred from the study of child training alone and likewise child-training techniques should not be explained as derivatives of cultural themes. If the determinants of modal personality are to be identified and analyzed, the entire "circular system" must be examined.

Some further comments about the use of the statistical concept mode are necessary. The mode of a series of variations may represent but a small portion of the entire series. In a modern nation the discontinuities in the society are such that the modal behavior, or personality, gives an incomplete if not distorted picture. It appears that many of the national character students assume a higher degree of homogeneity of national culture than may actually be true.

The existence of caste, class, religious, ethnic, or geographic differences represent major discontinuities. There are, of course, many other factors in a complex industrialized society which tend to disturb the picture of a homogeneous national culture; however, it is class and geocultural areas which are of most concern.

PART TWO

ENGLISH AND AMERICAN
SOCIAL STRUCTURE:

Essays illustrating the analytical use of the concepts
class, status, and power

chapter four

CLASS, STATUS, AND POWER
IN ENGLAND*

It was pointed out in the previous section that there has been no consistent usage of the terms "class" and "status," and that both Marx and Weber associated "power" with class consciousness and political party. Weber also could conceive of status-based parties. In order that the following discussion may proceed without producing more ambiguities, working definitions are stated at the outset.

Social classes are defined as dynamic or potentially dynamic quasi-groups which may or may not become social movements (power groups which may alter the societal status quo), depending upon the degree of solidarity generated by the conscious acceptance of common interests, ideologies, and life chances by the "members" of such quasi-groups. Social classes are historically associated with property relations, and the sharing of a common economic orientation is still the primary factor in the class situation.

Social status groups are defined as hierarchical strata in society, based on levels of prestige and a specific style of life. The strata are dynamic only in respect to interaction of a competitive nature between them and within the societal status quo. Social status groups are associated with differentiation of social roles, and the social estimation of honor attached to these roles is the primary factor in the status situation.

Social power is defined as "the ability to introduce force into social situations." The locus of social power is in intergroup

---

* From *Social Forces,* Vol. XXX, No. 2, 1951.

relations and may be expressed in formal or informal organization
or in the unorganized community. The effectiveness of power is
associated with the numbers of people involved, the degree of
organization and the availability of resources. When these factors
are so arranged as to represent latent force, a power situation
exists. Social power may be attached to status and usually
generates prestige. It may be used either to maintain the societal
status quo or to disrupt it.[1]

Although these concepts—class, status, and power—may be
separately defined to facilitate their use in the description and
analysis of a society, they are as realities in society—to the extent that they are realities—complexly interrelated. As has been
indicated, a social class may form a social movement and thereby
through organization, numbers, and resources, develop a power
situation to which prestige attaches. Historically, in England,
the landed gentry as a power group was largely displaced by
the bourgeoisie following the commercial and industrial revolutions. In recent years there has been some evidence of a further
shift of power accompanying the quasi-socialist revolution and
the establishment of a welfare state.

A change of power relations in a society is accompanied or
followed by changes in the social estimation of honor attached
to the group which has created a new, or assumed direction of
a previously existing power situation. The group or class which
has come into power gains prestige, and its social status is raised.
This status gain is not acquired through individual or group
behavior per se, but is a function of the offices which members
of the group now fill in a newly created power situation or as
functionaries in previously existing social institutions.

The shift of status honor which follows changes in the power
situation is never complete. If the landed aristocracy is denied its
political power, it may, for a period of time, retain its property
to which prestige is attached. If it loses its land, family remains
and a distinctive style of life may be perpetuated. If the noble
families are broken up by exogamous marriages, nothing remains
but tradition, and it should be added that tradition, particularly
in England, dies hard. The social history of England reveals the
long struggle of the landed gentry to maintain power and status

and the equally long struggle of the new merchant class to gain power and status. In the end, although the landed aristocracy relinquished practically all power, its status remained high— nourished by living tradition, myth, ritual, and symbol.

Thus, a certain stratum of society may survive and enjoy high status honor and at the same time have no corresponding social power. This is the position of the few holders of large estates and other remnants of the old gentry in England today. Since they are essentially a static and devitalized stratum of society, they come nearer to fitting the definition of a status group than that of a social class.

The loss of the landed gentry was the gain of the bourgeoisie. The bourgeoisie developed the solidarity which gave rise to class consciousness and fostered a social movement directed at altering the societal status quo in its own interests. It had a common economic orientation and it succeeded in producing political and economic ideologies which rationalized its economic activities. The bourgeoisie represented a dynamic class movement which rapidly acquired social power and the status honor attached to property and political office. As a class, however, in its early development, its power and status were mainly derived from the new forms of property relations, rather than from political office. As long as the state would not interfere with their economic interest, they were, on the whole, content to leave political office in the hands of the old aristocracy.

The industrial capitalists and the merchants formed the English bourgeoisie of the early industrial period. All the economic and political ramifications consequent upon the rise of this class cannot be discussed here. It should be pointed out, however, that the style of life of this class represented a greatly increased demand for various kinds of consumer goods. This expanded consuming power, stimulated by competition for higher status honor, brought into being new industries, new shops, new technicians, and new or expanded professional services. This expanding laissez-faire economy, however, resulted in the segmentation of the bourgeoisie.[2]

The nineteenth century, a period of economic prosperity and expansion, thus gave rise to a host of new occupational and professional groups. The salaried lower professions—teachers, nurses, supervisors, and engineers—as well as the clerks, managers, and technicians, increased in number. The free enterprise system fostered the establishment of many small businesses, and the same system permitted the growth of small business into large-scale trusts and monopolies.

The present composition of the "middle class" in England is difficult to determine. Gretton (1919), pointed out that historically it appeared that the middle class was ". . . so lacking in marked characteristics or qualities that it could only be described as lying between two other classes." However, he defined the middle class as ". . . that portion of the community to which money is the primary condition and the primary instrument of life."[3] He included in this group: merchants, capitalists (bankers, insurance and investment men), and professionals. He excluded landlords, peasants, shopkeepers, and artisans.

Carr-Saunders and Jones classified the population of England by industrial status and produced the following: (1) managerial, 6.4 percent; (2) operative, 86.7 percent; (3) workers on own account, 6.9 percent. The same authors presented a breakdown according to "kind of payment," as follows: wage earners, 76 percent; salaried, 14 percent; independent workers, 6 percent; and employers, farmers and professionals, 4 percent. In reference to the middle class, they say, ". . . it never was anything more than a heterogeneous assemblage of very diverse elements."[4]

Lewis and Maude see the middle class as composed of: businessmen and managers, higher public servants, the professions, the farmers, the shopkeepers and traders. The middle class, they think, makes up between 33.5 percent and 37.5 percent of the population.[5]

The Institute of Public Opinion conducted a poll in 1948, utilizing the question, "If you had to say what social class you belong to, which would it be?" The responses were as follows: Upper, 2 percent; Upper Middle, 6 percent; Middle, 28 percent; Lower Middle, 13 percent; Working, 46 percent; no reply, 5 percent.[6]

G. D. H. Cole discusses the problems of identifying and measuring the middle class and designates twelve occupational groups as "middle class." He concludes that the heterogeneous group which he has designated has as its chief common interest ". . . concern with the defense of economic and social inequality against leveling tendencies, which threaten either their incomes or their property, or those parts of the social structure which narrow the ways of entry into the better paid occupations, and thus keep down the competition for superior jobs."[7]

Ginsberg distinguishes between the new and the old middle class and recognizes the difficulties involved in considering "this heterogeneous mass as a single class." He says:

> The situation differs in different countries according to the degree of industrialism and the part played by agriculture, but nowhere do the middle classes possess a coherent policy in relation to the other groups. There is a certain amount of antagonism between the old middle class, whose position is threatened by the growth of large-scale methods of production and distribution, and the new middle-class to whom the newer developments provide ever fresh opportunities. Both new and old are divided within, in their attitude to the growing demand for the control of industry by the working classes; but though the middle classes are economically and politically divided, there is among them a certain approximation in social status, which, despite the presence of numerous gradations, marks them off from the working classes.[8]

These references would seem to justify the use of the loose term, "middle classes" in referring to this large portion of the society. The picture is further confused by the fact that the upper fringe of this group merges into the remnants of the old aristocracy and, among its lower portions, there is a tendency to identify with the working class.

It appears that the present "middle classes" have but little resemblance to the earlier bourgeoisie, which was a fairly well-unified group. Its unity came from a positive common interest which supplied the dynamics of a power group, whereas what unity exists in the "middle classes" of today is largely of a negative nature in defense of the economic basis of their style of life.[9] Furthermore, the several groups composing the "middle classes" have different economic bases—different sources of income in interest, fees, and salaries—and therefore do not share a common economic orientation which is the primary factor in the class situation. One may conclude that the present English "middle classes" do not constitute a social class in terms of the definition that has been proposed.

The contemporary "middle classes" can best be considered as a series of strata sharing, within very broad limits, a distinctive style of life. Great variation exists in the social power of the several strata in the series and, likewise, there are differences in the amount of social honor attached to them. (The distribution of power is further discussed below in relation to the working class.)

The identification of the working class does not present quite the difficulties which are involved in relation to the middle class. Historically the urban working class began to form a recognizable portion of the society following the introduction of new technical inventions for carding and spinning cotton. The process of enclosure, which had been proceeding for two hundred years, now increasingly drove workers from the land and, as the domestic system of manufacture gave way to the factory system, the industrial towns became the home of a fast-growing proletariat.[10]

The long struggle of this group against the social and economic conditions which accompanied the Industrial Revolution need only be mentioned here. It was these conditions which, in the long run, provoked a considerable degree of consciousness of their common position in the economic system. Enough solidarity was thus generated to bring about mass revolts of workers in the first half of the nineteenth century. Industrial action through trade unions representing the organized force of workers in mines and factories reached its height in 1834, but was suppressed by the government.

The Chartist movement represented fundamentally the same class interests but was an attempt to better its position through political action rather than by industrial conflict. Their petitions, however, were rejected and the Chartist movement fell to pieces. It was only after 1850, when the national economic situation had improved by control of world markets, that the workers were able to form stable trade unions which became an organized force. When combined with other working-class groups, they finally gave rise to the Labour Party.[11]

The unity of the working class was far from complete. The Marxist Socialist Democratic Federation was in ideological conflict with the main body of the trade union and Independent Labour Party movements at the same time that the "middle class" Fabian Society provided a part of the ideology upon which these movements were based. Nevertheless, this long struggle, which culminated in the British Labour Party, illustrates the action of a social class which came to function as a power group intent upon the modification of the societal status quo. As to the composition of the working class, Carr-Saunders and Jones, as pointed out previously, designate in their "industrial status" categories, 86.7 percent of the population as "operatives." In their categories based upon kind of payment, they estimate 76 percent of the population to be wage earners. It is also interesting to note that after Carr-Saunders and Jones have expressed serious doubts as to the existence of upper and middle classes in England, they say "It is true that the 'working class' remains . . . ," and point out that "This class is characterized by the weekly cash wage payment and by a greater degree of uncertainty about future employment than faces other members of the community."[12] They also point out that the working class has been so designated in legislation.

Tawney estimates that the working class composes three-quarters of the community, and points out that although it is made up of people of ". . . widely diverse incomes, economic positions, social conditions, personal interests and habits, types of culture, political opinions, and religious creed . . . ," it may be considered a social class ". . . from a limited economic angle, only in the sense that its members depend for their livelihood on the wage contract."[13]

The Institute of Public Opinion, as previously mentioned, found 46 percent of their respondents designating themselves as "working class," whereas Lewis and Maude estimate the working class to be between 62.5 percent and 66.5 percent of the population, and they would include skilled and unskilled manual

workers as well as the lower paid clerical workers.[14] G. D. H.
Cole considers wage payments:

> . . . the characteristic incomes of the working class, although
> many of the lower salaries, but also some of the higher, are
> negotiated by methods of collective bargaining closely akin to
> trade union wage-negotiations, and, in Great Britain at any rate,
> there is a growing tendency for the lesser salary-earners to join
> the Trades Union Congress and to regard themselves as belong-
> ing with, and in many cases to, the working class movement. Not
> only the shop assistant and the clerk, but also to an increasing
> extent, the scientific workers, the supervisor, and the Civil
> Servant, except at the highest levels, are on the whole, aligned
> with the manual workers against the profit-makers and the
> *rentiers*, when it comes to a question of the distribution of the
> national income or the development of the social services of the
> Welfare State.[15]

Ginsberg also considers wage payments to be the mark of the
working class. "The characteristics of this class are well marked.
Its members get their living by the sale of their labour for a
wage. . . ."[16]*

The working class in England clearly includes the main body
of wage workers, both skilled and unskilled. Generally speaking,
this quasi-group evidences a degree of solidarity through conscious acceptance of common interests, ideologies, and life
chances, and shares a common economic orientation. They share,
in a Marxist sense, similar positions in relation to the processes
of production. To this group may be added the "brain workers"
who consciously identify themselves with wage workers. Their
identification may be based upon a recognition of similar economic interests and life chances, or upon the acceptance of the
working-class ideology. Although it is true that the large body
of wage workers share a certain style of life, yet differences in
specific styles of life which may exist between unskilled workers,

---

* He indicates, however, that the working class ". . . may include border-
line cases (the so-called proletariod) of people who are not strictly wage
earners and who work on their own account, but whose independence
and security have so slight a foundation, that they are always on the verge
of joining the proletariat" (p. 167).

skilled artisans, trade union officials, and certain groups of intellectuals does not prevent them from being "members" of the working class. In other words, the class situation is determined by economic orientation and is solidified by a common ideology. It is not dependent upon a common style of life of the persons involved, although it is true that those persons being in the same class situation will, in all probability, share a generally similar style of life.

Now, the problem for consideration is: To what extent does the working class represent a power group in contemporary England? In other words, has there been a shift in the locus of power in the society and if so, what is the extent of the change?

To answer these questions would require a definitive study of the social, economic, and political structure and function of the society. In broad outline, however, the problem may be examined.

If the effectiveness of a power group is dependent upon numbers, organization, and resources,[17] these three aspects of the working class must be explored. As to numbers, the working class is by far the most numerous of the three "classes," representing roughly two-thirds to three-quarters of the population. ". . . the numerical preponderance of the wage-workers is obviously the first characteristic of the structure of English society, when it is regarded in its economic aspect, as an organization for the production of wealth."[18] The Labour Party, with its affiliated constituency parties, trade unions, socialist and cooperative societies, has a total membership of 5,716,947 (1949).[19] This political organization which polled nearly twelve million votes in 1945, is the strongest political force in England, although its majority is small.

Of course the Labour Party cannot be considered as identical with the working class. In fact, although there is some dissension within the party on this point, it is the avowed end of the party that it shall be, or indeed has already become, "a classless party"—"a truly national party." Nevertheless, its major support is from the working class.[20] As to resources, the Labour Party has a sizable annual income, the major portion of which comes from the trade unions in affiliation fees for their members.*

It has been largely, but not entirely, through the efforts of this political party, that a strictly constitutional quasi-socialist revolution has taken place. The establishment of the welfare state has by nationalization of basic industries, a progressive system of taxation and subsidies, and, through expanded social security, altered the power relations in the society.

It is only possible, considering the novelty of the present situation, and the paucity of reliable information, to make certain reasonable assumptions as to the meaning of these changes in terms of power. First, nationalization diminishes the power of private property per se. Second, the system of progressive taxation, particularly the increased death duties and food subsidies, tend to redistribute the national wealth. This redistribution is largely in income; there remains great concentration in ownership of private property.[21] Third, expanded social services also tend, indirectly, to redistribute the wealth as well as to increase the general well-being of low-income groups. Each of these processes, it is reasonable to assume, tends to diminish the power of certain sections of the "middle classes," and to increase the power of the working class. Changes in power relations are also related to the organization of the welfare state.

Max Weber could write of England in 1918: "The gentry has saved England from the bureaucratization which has been the fate of all continental states."[22] And in *Wirtschaft und Gesellschaft*, ". . . the advance [of bureaucratic structure] has been realized most slowly where older structural forms have been technically well developed and functionally adjusted to the requirements at hand. This was the case, for instance, in the administration of notables in England and hence England was the slowest of all countries to succumb to bureaucratization or, indeed, is still only partly in the process of doing so."[23]

---

* Union members may "contract out," that is, they may formally advise their unions that they do not wish to contribute to the political affiliation fund.

However, in the formal organization of the welfare state, bureaucracy is greatly expanded and thus it provides a possible avenue by which social power may be transformed into authority: ". . . the manifold tasks of the so-called 'policy of social welfare' operate in the direction of bureaucratization, for these tasks are, in part, saddled upon the state by interest groups and, in part, the state usurps them, either for reasons of power policy or for ideological motives."[24]

A fourth reasonable assumption is, then, that bureaucratic structure has expanded, and that, with this development, not only has the bureaucratic official gained social honor, but that the functioning of the bureaucracy has resulted, to some extent, in the leveling of status honor throughout the society.[25] This results from what Weber has called ". . . the characteristic principle of bureaucracy: the abstract regularity of the execution of authority which is the result of the demand for 'equality before the law' ('Fair shares for all' of the Labour Party) in the personal and functional sense—hence, the horror of 'privilege.' . . . "[26] Thus, bureaucracy, which has accompanied the welfare state in England, has tended toward the "leveling of the governed" and at the same time, has increased the status honor of the "bureaucratically articulated group."

The articulated group—the officials and functionaries in this case—is heterogeneous. It includes members of both the working class and of the "middle classes." Due largely to the existence of an insufficient number of trained personnel, many of the bureaucratic offices were and are occupied by the same men who previously held power on the basis of ownership of property or as an official in a bureaucratically organized private industry.

It has been assumed that the existence of a large number of such men in the new bureaucracy has had the effect of negating any real gain of power by the working class. G. D. H. Cole says, for example, ". . . in the main, the class structure is left as it was: the same sorts of people hold the same relative social positions as before, and accordingly, a high proportion of those in the key positions are hostile to socialism. There is no unloosening of new enthusiasms among the common people, and no rapid emergence of a new leadership."[27]

Schumpeter has pointed out ". . . that the socially necessary functions that succeed one another in historical time are related in important respects—administrative skill, resoluteness, and the ability to command are vital to any leading position."[28] Thus, a ruling class in one regime has certain prerequisites which will facilitate its assuming power in a new social structure. Its success, however, depends upon its ability to adjust to the new situation.[29]

If bureaucracy is an impersonal apparatus which functions from the top down, that is, if the various officials and functionaries are controlled by the nature of their offices and all policy emanates from the very top of the hierarchy,[30] then the assumption that the presence of a large number of anti-socialists in the bureaucratic structure has prevented a shift in power relations, or succeeded in perpetuating the power of certain groups of the "middle classes," is untenable.*

The tendency of a displaced class to assume new positions of power, discussed by Schumpeter, is of course, true. However, in England, the transition involves ideological changes of such magnitude that the old "middle class" ruling group is, on the whole, unable to accommodate itself to the "new society."†

One may conclude that a real shift in power—from certain groups of the "middle classes" to the working class—has taken place in England. The extent of this change in the power situation is undetermined. The gain in power has yielded the prestige of office and thereby increased the social estimation of honor enjoyed by the working class. The welfare state has brought about changes in the ownership and control of property and in the distribution of income which has been, on the whole, somewhat more favorable to the working class than to other groups in the society. The functioning of the welfare state through

---

* The writer interprets Professor Cole's phrase, "a high proportion of those in key positions" as referring to key men in the bureaucratic mechanism, and not to men in a position to formulate basic political and economic policy.

† The non-nationalized sectors of the society are very extensive, and provide wide areas for the exercise of power in traditional free enterprise fashion.

extended bureaucratic organization has tended toward a leveling of status honor in the society by the denial of privilege, and the same structure has provided the prestige of office to more members of the working class than had been the case in the previous regime. Yet, although a large proportion of such bureaucratic offices is filled by members of other "classes," who thereby also acquire such status as the offices may yield, power relations are not affected unless or until these "middle class" groups attain to policy-making positions. This could come about either through the process of accommodation of those groups to the "new society" or through the process of conflict which would necessitate generating a degree of solidarity of interests, to form the basis of a dynamic class movement.

At present, the working class in England is the recipient of a large degree of power, and it has a higher social status than it has ever before enjoyed. Office and vocation—social function— are tending slowly to replace property and wealth as determinants of social status. Nevertheless, traditional status distinctions survive which have no corresponding social function. The persistence of customary social honor appropriate to a power situation which has been significantly altered, has created a lag between social power and accorded status. This lag has both denied the working class status fully commensurate with its function, and has, to a certain extent, blinded the working class to the full realization of the existing situation.

chapter five

THE UNITED STATES: CLASS OR
STATUS SOCIETY?*

Archibald MacLeish once said that there are only two classes
of people—those who divide people into classes and those who
don't; it would appear that in the United States there are fast
becoming two classes of sociologists—those who do and those
who don't. George Simpson's statement of 1939 seems apropos:
"The term class has assumed an importance in contemporary
social theory in inverse proportion to its clarity as a scientific
instrument for the investigation of the phenomena with which
it purports to deal."[31] Some of this lack of clarity is due to
different conceptions of the nature of the phenomena under
consideration. At least a portion of the difficulty may arise
from the failure to differentiate for conceptual purposes social
status groups and classes. The working definitions which were
stated in the preceding paper are employed here in an attempt
to answer the question, Is the United States a class- or status-
based society?

The tendency to define classes as hierarchically arranged
prestige groupings and the prevalence of the use of multiple
criteria of such classes, usually summarized in terms of social
status or prestige, may account for some of the confusion. The
relative neglect of sociological studies in terms of the power
relations existing between economic interest groups has tended
to overemphasize the importance of prestige in the class situation.

After a critique of current literature on social stratification,
Pfautz concludes: "In the conceptualizations of status and class

---

* From *Sociology and Social Research*, Vol. XL, No. 5, 1956.

there has been an obvious preoccupation with prestige to the neglect of power."[32] The accuracy of this assertion is widely accepted. The definition of class in terms of status and prestige is so common that it seems likely that many undergraduates in sociology conceive of social stratification as being confined to such considerations as "keeping up with the Joneses in Jonesville" or "who associates with whom in Zenith."

These studies of status relations in selected communites, on the whole, have been carefully done. They represent a legitimate area of research and have made a contribution to sociology. Just why so much attention should have been given to the prestige aspects of stratification to the neglect of other aspects, is a problem which cannot be adequately dealt with here. However, several explanations may be postulated: the influence of Warner and his associates, the development of research techniques which are applicable to such studies, and the conscious or unconscious avoidance of Marxian notions of class.

Generally speaking, the findings of these status studies have been interpreted in one of two ways: (1) that a well-defined hierarchy of status groups (frequently referred to as social classes) exists in the community studied, there being five or six levels which form as many easy steps up or down, or (2) that some people have more prestige than others but that there are no well-defined groupings—the various levels forming a continuum from low to high.

These findings are meaningful as long as they are interpreted in terms of status and prestige. It seems doubtful that the existence of clear-cut status groups can be demonstrated in the United States. Even the postulation of distinct status groups or a status system in the United States would seem to be incompatible with the historical-cultural development of the society. The United States experienced no period of real feudalism with its well-defined estates easily identifiable by appropriate status symbols. The absence of feudalism, as Lipset and Bendix have pointed out, does not mean a lack of status distinctions in the society, but it did facilitate the development of a strong ideological equalitarianism in spite of the existing status differentials.[33] This equalitarian ideology, the belief in individualism and equality of opportunity, along with the natural wealth of the country and a relatively high degree of mobility, militated against the development of a status-based society.

Regional and subcultural development gave rise to different criteria of high and low status in different parts of the country. Family background was all-important in the South, association with shipbuilding and the maritime industry in New England, and one's facility with firearms in the "old West." No universal symbols of status—not even wealth—have ever developed. Sjoberg and others have pointed out that with the rise of mass production, the availability of certain consumer goods which have come to have prestige value tended to blur status distinctions. Also, a part of the manual working class receives sufficient money income to place it, in relation to some aspects of life, on a level with the middle class.[34] From de Tocqueville to Bryce to Laski, Europeans have repeatedly observed that it is difficult to identify the shop girl or to distinguish the clerk from the banker in America.[35]

It is not surprising, then, that research studies reveal no status systems per se—no discrete prestige groupings in a community, much less in the society as a whole.

The question in the minds of some social scientists is: What relation do these findings have to the question of whether or not classes exist in the United States? Considerable confusion is present on this point. Some have concluded on the basis of these prestige-oriented studies that there is no class system in the United States and that we should stop talking about it.[36] It can be maintained, however, that the conclusions drawn from such studies should be confined to hypotheses concerning the nature of, or the existence of, a status system in contradistinction to a class system.

It seems to those who take the second view that there are certain advantages in differentiating between status groups and classes.[37] If the concept of class includes status, prestige, style of life, life chances, as well as power and economic factors, then it is impossible to study the relations between these concepts. On the other hand, the relationship is not consistent. For example, some occupational groups have great prestige and little power and vice versa. Some classes have power which is not accompanied by comparable prestige.[38]

The use of what might be called the historical-classical conception of social class might avoid some of the confusion which has characterized the prestige concept of class. In the historical-classical frame of reference, classes would be composed of people who find themselves in similar relationships to the economic processes and would include individuals and groups of varying prestige. Such classes are society-wide, dynamic or potentially dynamic power groups, composed of individuals who have a similar economic orientation. Whether or not they become power groups depends upon the degree of solidarity achieved through recognition of similar interests and acceptance of similar ideologies, as well as upon organization and the utilization of symbolic representations in achieving what are defined as desirable changes in the existing social structure. Such a conception of class would prove valuable in analyzing social change, in studying social movements and in analyzing problems of social control. It is a concept which might be useful in studying some of what Znaniecki calls the "large-scale problems" in sociology.[39]

The question which now arises is: Using this economically based potential power group approach to social class, do such classes exist in the United States? Here, also, we may find a division of opinion. It may be suggested, however, that the power group or potential power group concept may, considering the nature of the larger society, offer a more fruitful approach than has the prestige-status group definition. The Lynds found it useful in Middletown. Mills seems to identify the business class and the working class in this frame of reference. Much has been written about organized labor and big business as power groups.

Some would deny the existence of a working class with proletarian implications. The proletariat which is associated with the rise of capitalism has been characterized as a free working class, largely without property, that lives by the sale of its labor for wages. It seems as if it would be difficult to deny the existence of such a class in the United States, even though it may have undergone what appears to be an external "bourgeoisiazation."

We may have the most unproletarian proletariat that ever existed, but it is still a proletariat—wage workers and most salaried workers, dependent upon the sale of their labor in the market and propertyless except for the ownership of the hollow symbols of the bourgeoisie. They have, during times of economic prosperity, a relatively high standard of living; and because of the lack of well-defined, traditional status symbols in the United States, they can at times, in a highly secondary society, "pass themselves off" as middle-class. This is a façade made possible by the mass production of which they are a part. Possession of middle-class symbols—money to spend, relatively high social status, even prestige—does not, some would argue, change their established relationship to existing economic processes and therefore does not change their class. Their general economic orientation is still the same.

It is true that only a part of the proletariat has formulated a very realistic conception of their class position. Only a small part of them subscribe to class ideology,[40] but being objectively in the same class situation, all workers are potentially class conscious—a potential power group.

The business class, or possibly "big business" would be more accurate, is relatively easy to identify in our society, although there may be quibbling about the lower limits of such a group. This class is composed of those whose income is derived largely from the ownership of property. Finding themselves in the same relationship to economic processes, members of this group tend to have similar economic interests and to subscribe to a common ideology. It would seem difficult to deny that this group wields considerable power in political and economic matters, in the light of our knowledge of big business organizations.

The middle class, that large group which Gretton (1919)[41] pointed out was historically so lacking in marked characteristics or qualities that it could only be described as lying between two other classes, may also be defined in terms of power. In reference to the middle class, however, it is the lack of power that is significant. Mills thus considers the middle class as a kind of power vacuum.[42] It would seem, however, that this large and admittedly ill-defined class can also be considered either as a potential power group itself or as lending its latent power under certain circumstances to either the working class or the big business class.

The important factor in regard to each class in this frame of reference is its potential for forming an action group oriented toward either changing the societal status quo or maintaining it. Morris Ginsberg has pointed out that "classes are not actual but potential groups; not in themselves associations, with specific functions, but they may form the material for associations, for example, political parties."[43]

The question remains as to whether or not such classes form a "class system." The connotations of *system* are the existence of some form of interaction or interdependence between parts. It would seem reasonable to allege the existence of such a relationship between classes. The pragmatic observation of the existence of, and the successes of, the capitalistic system would seem to verify such a relationship between classes.

Even though classes have been defined here in what may be interpreted as quasi-Marxian terms, the relationship existing between them in the United States cannot be defined in terms of opposition—class conflict—with the goal of revolutionary changes in the economic processes or in the complete transference of power. Rather it would appear that interaction and interdependence existing between classes in this country could be better described as antagonistic cooperation. The objective of these potential power groups, when and if they become action groups, is to bring about change in the sense of modification of existing socioeconomic arrangements, rather than to establish a new set of relationships.*

---

* The writer would like to point out that he, too, has used the term *social class* rather loosely in some research reports. When social class has been used to refer to occupational prestige groups, the referent has been made explicit and the emphasis has been on social in contradistinction to economic or political or just plain class.

PART THREE

SOCIAL CLASS STUDIES—ENGLAND:
Illustrating the relation between class and status
in a changing society

chapter six

THE CONTEMPORARY
WORKING-CLASS SITUATION

"Working-class situation" as used in this essay includes the phenomena of class, status and power as they have previously been delineated. For the purposes of discussion, it again seems desirable to separate social status factors from economic well-being and power, thus making it possible to observe differential positions and movement in relation to these criteria of social standing.

Common academic English conceptions of the working class[1] often support the traditional usage of the term in referring to that portion of the population characterized on the economic side by manual labor and wage payment. It is frequently assumed that the workers' relation to the processes of production determines, to a large extent, other components in the working-class situation. The working class is thus seen as evidencing a degree of separateness and solidarity through sharing common interests, ideologies, and life chances. Estimates as to the size of the working class vary from about 60 to 75 percent of the population. To this group, which is characterized by manual labor, may be added the "brain workers" who consciously identify themselves with the working class by the recognition of similar economic interests and life chances, or by the acceptance of the working-class ideology. The power aspect of class rests upon the proposition that the portion of the population which finds itself in the working-class situation presents a potential or actual power group in the society.

By focusing attention upon the *class situation*, one may avoid the possible negation of the analysis by particularistic conceptions of class, i.e., class is determined by one's relation to the processes of production; class is style of life, social status in the community; class is a potential or actual power group in the society. Assessing the working-class situation then becomes a problem in analyzing the existing relationships and interaction between *economic factors* (amount of real income in money and services, source of income, and patterns of consumption), *power factors,* and *status factors* (prestige, social honor, style of life, etc.)[2]

Economic Factors

One may assume that changes in economic factors are subject to the most objective analysis and that previous study has verified a substantial change which may be described as marked improvement in economic well-being. In fact, England has a long tradition of surveys concerned with the economic condition of the working class. Observations and reports go back several centuries. However, it was not until the end of the nineteenth century and the early twentieth century that systematic studies were made. The work of Charles Booth, B. Seebohm Rowntree, the Webbs, and Arthur Bowley revealed conditions of widespread hardship and poverty among the working people. Largely through the efforts of these men, poverty came to be regarded as a social evil. They built up a fund of social facts, collected by respectable techniques and subjected to a degree of quantification, which marked the end of the seamy society created by the Industrial Revolution and the beginning of what has come to be called the welfare state.[3]

By employing a rather tenuous method of comparing findings of these surveys through time one may, nevertheless, substantiate an uneven but continuous improvement in the working-class situation in relation to the remainder of society. For example, in 1889, Booth estimated that approximately 30 percent of the working-class population of London were living in poverty. Forty years later, using somewhat comparable criteria, Bowley found only 9 percent below the poverty line. Rowntree's study of the conditions of the working class in York in 1936 revealed 14.2 percent at the poverty level and a restudy in 1950 found that poverty was nearly nonexistent (.37 percent).[4] Poverty has theoretically been eliminated in Britain through the functioning of the welfare state. Expanded social services are such that a minimum subsistence (above what is usually defined as poverty) is provided for all in case of need, regardless of the nature of factors which contributed to indigence.

Other studies indicate that the proportion of the national income received by the working class has continually increased over a long period of time. Patrick Colquhoun in 1814 estimated that the working classes (75 or 80 percent of the population) received less than one-third of the national income.[5] Working class income rose to 42 percent in 1880 and fell to 36 percent by 1913. As a result of the policy of redistribution of income of the welfare state, it is now estimated that 65 to 70 percent (depending upon which categories are included) of the national income is consumed in wages and salaries.[6] It should be pointed out, however, that property ownership in land and industrial capital remains highly concentrated.[7] Nevertheless, on the side of economic well-being in wages and material possessions, there is no question concerning the continually improving position of the working class. Nor is there any doubt about the present favorable position of that class as a direct result of national policy. An exaggerated and biased appraisal of these economic gains has frequently led to the denial of the existence of a working class in England today.

Data collected by the writer in connection with a research project in Tewkesbury, Gloucestershire, in 1957 (*infra*) shows how people in a community may arrive at the conclusion that no working class exists. Each of twenty judges indicated by a ranking procedure that factory workers in the community had, during the past twenty years, moved from the lower working or upper working classes into the lower middle or upper middle classes when social class was determined by economic well-being. It was not uncommon to hear the expression from middle-class interviewees: "There are no working classes in England today." Some sections of the middle class who resent recent changes tend, in a masochistic fashion, to exaggerate these changes in order to dramatize their own position. They believe that they have borne a large and disproportionate share of the cost of the welfare

state and that they have not received a proportionate share of
expanded social services. G. D. H. Cole says on this point: "The
high level of taxation on middle and higher incomes which is
irreversible in view of the commitment of all parties to the expansion of the social services, involves squeezing of the spending
power of those sections of the middle classes whose gross incomes
are least expansible—especially the salary earners outside industry and the possessors of smallish unearned incomes. . . . These
prospects, however, fall a long way short of threatening any
important section of the middle classes with impending ruin or
even serious social decline."[8]

Power Factors

Social power refers to the latent or actual ability to introduce
force into social situations. Social classes may be power groups
in this sense. Bierstedt has pointed out that power is related to
the number of people involved, the degree of organization and
the availability of resources.[9]

Considering the existing formal and informal associations of
the working class with the Labour Party, it seems reasonable to
consider that the working class may be a power group in the
society. The working-class movement in the broadest sense, however, has suffered from the loss of working-class values associated
with an independent social movement. It is true that the trade
unions and the Labour Party are stronger than they ever were
before, but parallel groups in the labor movement—the consumers'
cooperatives, the workers' education system,[10] insurance societies,
sports clubs and holiday associations, are all on the decline.[11]

The Labour Party itself may suffer from increased attrition
through upward mobility. In fact, as this attrition becomes more
selective, through the equalization of educational opportunity,
the loss may become more serious. Some leaders of the Labour
Party have already shown concern that this process may weaken
future leadership. They fear that the loss may become greater
as the traditional working-class culture becomes less identifiable
with the attenuation of the economic struggle. The Labour Party
has, of course, always included among both its leaders and fol-
lowers, many persons who, on the basis of either social status or

economic well-being, would be placed in the middle or upper classes. It seems likely that the Labour Party gains through intellectual identification will equal or exceed losses through social mobility accompanied by ideological defection.*

There would seem to be but little doubt, then, about the English working class, as it is identified with and through the trade unions, structurally related to the Labour Party, functioning as a power group in the society. The power situation is sometimes exaggerated, as has been the economic improvement, in support of the idea that the working class no longer exists—it is the "ruling class" when the Labour Party is in power.†

Status Factors

Social status tends to rise with increased economic well-being and with the acquisition of power, but there is no one-to-one relationship between social status and economic well-being, nor between social status and power. Status and prestige tend to lag behind economic and power changes. This is fundamentally because prestige is bound up with institutional values in the society, which form the basis of the estimation of social honor attributed to persons and groups occupying differentiated role and status positions. A new status-prestige position is not self-engendered, but rather it is "granted" by society and this is dependent upon the modification of existing value systems.

One avenue to higher status which does not require modification of societal values is through occupying offices in governmental or other bureaucracies which are highly regarded in reference to the existing values and thereby lend their prestige to the holder of the office. As more working-class persons fill such offices in trade unions, nationalized industries, the Labour Party,

---

* This assumption is based upon the fact that the principles and objectives of the welfare state are now widely accepted by members of all classes and the further acceptance of socialist ideology and practice in the expansion of the welfare state seems highly probable.

† In 1950, when I was at the London School of Economics, a young student asked me the nature of my research. I said that I was interested in studying social classes in England, and he replied, "It is a pity, but you have come too late!"

and in the government itself, their improved social status will be reflected upon the whole working class. However, only a small number of workers will actually attain such position, status, and security. The mass of the working class, having experienced rather rapid changes in important aspects of the class situation, is apt to be characterized by a certain amount of uncertainty and insecurity. The internal, old working-class criteria of status and prestige are no longer applicable and the broader external definitions in relation to societal values have been disturbed. As Hoggart has pointed out in relation to the contemporary English working class, the old class culture characterized by "self-respect," tolerance, personal and concrete relationships, "an oral tradition," common speech, folk art and a host of folkways recognized as expected ways of behaving, has degenerated.[12]

Much effort is expended by the contemporary working class in trying to vindicate a new status, even though no one knows precisely what it is. In this process, there is a tendency to "denigrate work and applaud income,"[13] to display status symbols and to become uncritical in acceptance of the social and economic system. They seem to form a "cult of gratitude,"[14] and at the same time to forget about the struggles of the working class in the past.

It has frequently been pointed out that such a group "in transition" is particularly susceptible to the external forces brought to bear upon it through mass communication. Hoggart has described what he thinks is happening to the English working class as a result of mass communication media. The working-class newspapers, "spicy magazines," "sex and violence novels," popular songs, juke boxes, low grade moving pictures—all of these are filling the working-class cultural void and will soon obliterate the old working class as a culture group. The fact that the working class no longer suffers from harsh economic pressures and therefore has a lessened class consciousness—"feeling of belonging"—makes it easier to merge working-class people and a portion of the middle classes into a culturally characterless class—the emerging "classless class" of "flat-faced men."[15]

As in the case of the economic and power factors, one may, by pointing to signs of developing anomie in the area of social status and style of life of the working class, conclude that there is no working class in England—as a fairly distinct status-culture group. Hoggart begins his book by saying, "It is often said that there are no working classes in England now, that a bloodless revolution has taken place, that has so reduced social differences that already most of us inhabit an almost flat plain, the plain of the lower middle classes. I can see the truth in such a statement, within its proper context. . . ."[16]

Conclusions

From this kind of study, based upon observation, participation, and the interpretation of the findings of others, it would seem that, of the three major factors in the working-class situation, changes in economic and power relationships can be substantiated and described with some degree of certainty. The third factor, social status and what is implied by "style of life," are less easily analyzed. The problem, as has been pointed out, centers around social evaluation of occupational roles, particularly those involving manual labor. The traditional evaluation has come under attack as being socially unjustified. It is seen as perpetuating privilege based upon wealth or property ownership and is thus considered essentially dysfunctional. Socialists and others call for equal distribution of opportunity and a closer association between social function and social honor.

As educational[17] and occupational selection become based upon "more nearly equal" opportunity, and result in a closer association between ability and occupation, the heirarchy becomes less assailable as representing unjustified privilege. Improved selection tends to rationalize the existing differential estimation of social honor attached to occupations. Thus the high prestige of certain occupations and low prestige of others is re-enforced and the gap between them takes on more social significance.

To implement and extend the socialists' concept "parity of esteem" in relation to the hierarchy of occupations becomes a problem of redefinition of traditional value systems through deliberate public policy. Although tenable, this is obviously a long-term proposition. In the meantime, the social status position of the working class is ambiguous and an unduly large amount of effort will be expended by workers in an attempt to gain status recognition. At the same time, the insecurity implicit in the situation leaves the mobile group open to the debilitating influences of mass communication which may negate the whole process of achieving social status position comparable with their existing economic and power positions.

chapter seven

THE MIDDLE CLASS

There was no place for a middle class in Marx's conception of the class struggle. He thought that an essential characteristic of capitalism was to reduce all classes to two—the capitalist property owners and the propertyless proletariat. The struggle for power would be fought out between these two—and the working class would be the victor.

The property-owning class was usually referred to as the bourgeoisie. When Marx used the term "middle classes" they were pictured as a heterogeneous group composed of managers, supervisors, independent craftsmen, and shopkeepers, technicians, professionals, etc. They were usually referred to as the *petite bourgeoisie*. At the upper levels the *petite bourgeoisie* were considered to be the pawns of the capitalists and at the lower level they were seen as struggling workers who were certain to recognize, in time, that their interests were allied with those of the working class. Whatever middle class existed would be "ground out" between the two great antagonistic classes, the bourgeoisie and the proletariat.

At the time Marx was formulating these conceptions he was living in England in the midst of the development of a middle class of significant proportions. Industry was expanding; large industrial enterprises were being formed as joint stock companies. Both the technique of manufacture and the organization of factories necessitated the assistance of men who were neither owners of capital nor wage workers in the ordinary sense. They were a middle class. As this group became larger, their purchasing power increased. They required the services of professionals—doctors, lawyers, architects, artists, and teachers. They represented a growing consuming group, not only for professional services, but for all kinds of consumer goods. The middle class, despite its mixed character and general lack of uniform economic orientation, began to take on a somewhat distinctive way of life. "Apothecaries, attorneys, and the top layers of the teaching profession turned into a sort of middle-class gentlemen, and came much nearer in social status to barristers, clergymen and army officers—the old trilogy of gentlemanly professions."[18]

The new professions such as civil engineers, technicians, industrial managers and supervisors were in a rather ambiguous position in regard to social standing. They were above the workers and below the gentlemanly stratum.

The peculiar function of the English "public" school at this time was, among other things, to make gentlemen not only out of the sons of industrialists but out of all the boys who came under their influence. And, among these were representatives of the new middle class. As these schools increased in number, and as more managers, technicians, and others had the money to secure "places" for their sons, the manners, speech, and general outlook of the aristocracy was more widely disseminated among the middle classes.

Marx could not realize the importance of expanded popular education and the extension of the right to vote. Through these means social reforms were accomplished which lessened the "misery of the workers" and established a socially significant middle class.

It can, of course, be argued that although the middle class developed a distinctive way of life and might be considered socially significant, nevertheless it remained relatively powerless. The power remained with the *grande bourgeoisie* and with the rising proletariat. In more general terms, however, it seems clear that:

> . . . middle-class influence has been waxing and not waning (even) in the United States, despite the very advanced stage of American capitalist development. . . . It is not, as Marx prophesied, being driven down into the proletariat by the development of capitalism: on the contrary, advancing capitalism has shown itself exceedingly favorable to its multiplication, and declining capitalism, where we have examples of it, seems to drive the middle groups towards Fascism rather than towards the acceptance of the status of proletarians.[19]

In England today the middle classes probably make up about 30 to 35 percent of the population.[20] This estimate utilizes an occupational approach to class which represents economic orientation and a certain social status. Lewis and Maude include businessmen and managers, higher public servants, the professionals, the farmers, the shopkeepers and the traders.[21] Cole has composed a similar, but more detailed grouping of middle-class occupations:

(a) The main body of heads of private businesses, or of active partners or directors in businesses, except the greatest, concerned with manufacture or wholesale trading, or with other commercial or financial occupations.

(b) The main body of salaried administrators, managers, technicians, and accountants in similar types of business, including businesses publicly or cooperatively owned; and the higher salaried officers of a wide range of institutions and societies, from political parties to Trade Unions or Trade Associations to philanthropic, educational, and cultural bodies.

(c) The members of the principal recognized professions, whether salaried or working as consultants and remunerated by professional fees; including medical men, lawyers, ministers of religion, officers of the armed services, the upper ranges of the teaching profession, and the upper and middle ranges of the artistic and industrial professions.

(d) The higher and middle grades of the Civil Service, the Local Government service, and of other public or semi-public administrative services; and the corresponding grades of "voluntary" social service employees.

(e) The big and middle shop keepers, garage keepers, hotel keepers; and also the analogous groups of employed managers, accountants, and other officers employed by joint stock companies operating in these fields.

(f) The large and middle farmers and with them the relatively small numbers of managerial salaried workers employed on big farms.

(g) The unoccupied *rentiers*, living on unearned incomes, except the largest and some of the smallest. . . .

(h) Full-time students who have embarked on higher education at a university or comparable level, but have not completed their education, including students drawn from working-class households.

(i) More doubtfully, the main body of clerks, typists and other non-manual workers whose work falls below the managerial or recognized professional level.

(j) Still more doubtfully, the members of certain lesser professions, such as nursing, the lower ranges of school teaching and the less recognized social service occupations.

(k) Most doubtfully of all, the main body of shop assistants, warehouse workers, postal workers other than clerks and minor institutional officials.

(l) Just possibly, persons belonging to the lower supervisory grades in industry, transport, and other types of businesses, but falling below the managerial grades.[22]

There is a considerable difference of opinion about the contemporary position of the middle classes in England. The division is along ideological and class lines. For purposes of this discussion Lewis and Maude[23] will illustrate the Tory-middle-class view and Cole[24] the socialist-working-class view. This is, of course, an oversimplification, because the split is not that clear. Many middle-class people are members of the Labour Party and would agree with Cole and other socialist spokesmen. Some workers, particularly the very lowest in economic and social status, would support the Tories.

Lewis and Maude are not sociologists,* but they take what may be called essentially a functionalist view of society. They think that classes are not only necessary but that the middle class is more necessary than is any other class. They talk about ". . . . 'natural differences of function' . . . and . . . of a 'natural harmony' of interests. . . ."[25] Lewis and Maude insist that the "natural function" of the middle class be maintained—or rather restored—in order to save English society from dissolution. The natural function of the middle class is stated as being "to provide most of their nation's [the authors say that this also applies to the United States] brains, leadership and organizing ability, and they are the main vehicle for the transmission of the essential national culture."[26] The authors see in England the destruction of

---

* Roy Lewis is editor of *Future*, a British business magazine, and Angus Maude, a graduate of Oxford, is an economist and Conservative member of Parliament.

a special middle-class "quality and tradition of life." The middle class is losing or has already lost its educational advantage—many do not have an income which is sufficient to send their children to "public" schools.[27] It has lost its servants[28] and may lose a fancied monoply on "the English way of life."

This dire situation is the result of an "assault" upon the middle-class way of life by social and economic change consequent upon the establishment of a welfare state. The contention is that the costs of the welfare state in expanded social services, education, and health falls disproportionately hard upon the middle classes. They see the changes wrought by the welfare state as a "leveling down," not "leveling up" as the socialists maintain. What they seem to be saying is that we, the middle classes (say, 35 percent of the population), in the old days before higher taxes and death duties, usually could purchase the kind of education desired and the kind of medical care needed, so although now we have public education for all and free medical care, this is no great advantage to us. It appears to them doubtful that the moral and ethical considerations involved in broadening the opportunities for education and health offset the loss of certain "spiritual" and cultural beliefs and values of the middle class.

> The question whether the "squeezing" of the middle classes since 1939 has resulted in a net profit or loss to the nation as a whole is thus not easy to answer. To conclude that the undoubted benefits which have accrued to the poorer sections of the community [60 to 65 percent of the population] provide full compensation—morally and economically—for the losses sustained by the middle classes is not to answer the question. For we have suggested that these middle-class losses are beginning to set up chains of secondary reactions whose effects on the well-being of all classes . . . may be very serious. . . . What is likely to be the outcome of the . . . struggle—a struggle as much for beliefs as for material advantage. . . ?[29]

Lewis and Maude, in the end, are confident, "But England will somehow manage to remain a middle-class nation." They point out that "England now has no aristocracy, no upper class to take the lead. . . ." And that Socialist reforms have been middle-class inspired. It appears that they thereby find some solace—even if

the worst comes to pass: ". . . labour movements—even those far
to the Left—must always be middle class. . . ."[30] They end their
discussion by expressing the hope (fully in keeping with their
implicit functionalist frame of reference) that,

> Yet the vast—perhaps irresistible—weight of middle class pressure
> will continue to be applied towards the achievement of a state
> of affairs idealized by Palmerston: 'We have shown the example
> of a nation in which every class of society accepts with cheerful-
> ness the lot which providence has assigned it, while at the same
> time each individual of each class is constantly trying to raise
> himself in the social scale . . . by preserving good conduct and
> by steady and energetic exertion of the moral and intellectual
> qualities with which his Creator has endowed him.'[31]

G. D. H. Cole is a sociologist, of a kind—that is, of a kind that
is encountered more frequently in England and on the continent
than in the United States. He is a social historian, an economist,
and a social political theorist.* Cole thinks of social classes as
fundamentally antagonistic groups. He sees classes as the basis
for invidious social and economic distinction and as resulting in
an unequal distribution of objective privilege. For example, he
says of the contemporary middle class: ". . . a very large proportion of the heterogeneous groups that make up the middle classes
have a common concern with the defence of economic and social
inequality. . . ."[32] Classes are therefore essentially dysfunctional
in a democratic state. Cole can conceive, at least theoretically, of
a classless society. Although Cole thinks that the upper class has
ceased to exist "as a social class of really national significance,"
the middle classes are much in evidence. In his view, the welfare
state which, to say the least, hastened the demise of the aristocracy has, on the whole, caused the middle classes to expand and
prosper.

The intellectuals ". . . who have taken over the accents and
manners of the lesser gentlefolk of a century ago," are at the
present a much larger group than before; they come from widely
differing social origins; "they hold a much more stable position

---

* Professor Cole recently retired from the Chichele Chair of Social and
Political Theory at Oxford University.

in the social system; they are better paid and in the main live much less precariously than they used to do. . . ."[33] "Farmers, after a bad period in the second half of the nineteenth century and a slow recovery in the early years of the twentieth, have improved their economic position faster than any other considerable section of the occupied population." Shopkeepers have voiced some dissatisfaction. Hired labor is scarce and wages are relatively high. They are experiencing, however, fast turnover of stocks and they have fewer bad debts. Cole asserts that "shopkeepers . . . have done well as a class . . . there can be no doubt about their improved standards of income and security."[34] Farmers and shopkeepers make up the main body of middle-class "profit-makers" in contradistinction to "salary-earners." Although both groups have improved their economic position in the welfare state, they tend to vote Conservative.

Cole points out that the professions have greatly expanded in number. The social status of the professions is higher than it was previously. For example, he comments upon the medical profession:

> . . . whose social status was gradually changing. There had been [a hundred years ago—but remember that the welfare state had its beginnings a hundred years ago] a very wide gulf . . . in the medical profession between the small body of "physicians" and "physicians and surgeons" belonging to the Royal Colleges and the general run of practitioners, commonly called "apothecaries" and "surgeons" . . . most surgeons were merely licensed. Naval and military service were still common ways of picking up a qualification: only a small proportion of doctors held medical degrees of university standard. The "doctor" was not, as such, reckoned a gentleman.[35]

The welfare state, with the development of the National Health Service, has raised the standards of both medical education and medical practice. Financially, doctors are in a very favorable position.*

With the generally increased purchasing power and higher standards of living in the working class and with expanded

---

* See "Socialized Medicine," *infra*.

government responsibility, lawyers—solicitors and attorneys—prospered. "Teaching, except at university level and in a very few Public Schools, was a profession of very low prestige, and was much worse paid than now."[36]

The new professions associated with business and engineering such as accountants, bank managers, company managers and directors, civil engineers, and architects have never had the social status of the older professions. They are a salaried group, working for private industry or government, and have not fared as well as the "profit-makers." However, those associated with the nationalized industries have higher status and more economic security than was previously true. Social workers, nurses, and public health workers should also be included in this group.

These groups of "lesser professions" along with "clerks" of various kinds are sometimes referred to as the "blackcoats." Cole says, ". . . while the higher professions are busy improving their social and economic status . . . a host of new groups are rising from lower down the social scale . . . claiming to be recognized as professional workers. . . . These lesser professions give rise to a whole series of secondary *elites* within the broad group of professional occupations, and help to create new forms of social and economic stratification."[37]

Whereas the "profit-makers," as mentioned above, are apt to be affiliated with the Conservative party, "the 'salary-earners,' on the other hand, have provided many more converts to Trade Unionism and to political Labour, partly because salaries have become much more a matter for collective bargaining . . . but also because there is less educational and cultural difference than there used to be between most salary-earners, outside the higher professions, and the more skilled manual workers."[38] Cole points out, however, that the salary-earners are an "unstable political force."

In almost direct contradiction of Lewis and Maude, Cole concludes that:

Certainly the development of the Welfare State in Great Britain has not, in raising the living standards of the worst-off, thrown down the professional and managerial groups into the ranks of the proletariat or ground down shopkeepers and farmers into the mass of the underprivileged. On the contrary, it has made large concessions to the claims of doctors, shopkeepers, farmers, and small businessmen, giving them both bigger incomes and greater security than they have ever before enjoyed. . . . The rise of the working classes has not been, on the whole, at the expense of the middle classes: it has been much more a social leveling-up than a leveling-down, except for the really wealthy. Six years of Labour Government did not materially alter the social structure, except at the two extreme ends.[39]

In looking to the future of the middle classes, Cole says that "the road to economic equality, even if open, is much longer and more difficult than many Socialists used to suppose. . . ."[40] The modification of capitalism, a considerable amount of nationalized industry and the expansion of social services, does not eliminate differentials in income and social status. However, Cole points out that, as Marx had maintained, socialism tended to substitute income differences based upon function or personal service and capacity for differences based on ownership of property or of inherited wealth. Also, that as educational opportunities tend to become equalized, economic differences and status differences are more closely related to individual capacity rather than being socially inherited from the family. The conception of class includes social inheritance which is closely related to family. If the family loses its function in perpetuating status and class as a result of equal opportunities from primary to university, and if an expanding economy is maintained, "middle class" will become "merely a descriptive adjective, designating those in the middle, rather than a term defining a distinctive section of the population."[41] There would be in the Marxian sense no *petite bourgeoisie*.

These scholars—Lewis and Maude on the one hand and Cole on the other—present widely differing analyses of the contemporary English middle-class situation. They start from different ideological frames of reference; they see society in different terms; they conceptualize class differently, and they are interested in different problems.

Lewis and Maude are interested in maintaining the status quo. They are concerned with what has happened, or may happen to an idealized middle-class culture. In Max Weber's terms, they are defending a particular "style of life" with all its subjective elements: beliefs, values, manners, symbols. They conceive of class in status terms. Class status is acquired by the individual through either ascribed, inherited position or it is achieved through personal effort, by (as they quote Palmerston) preserving good conduct and by steady and energetic exertion of moral and intellectual qualities.

Cole sees class position largely as the result of impersonal social and economic forces. The direction and influence of these forces is determined by the existing structure of social institutions. The distribution of objective privilege is determined by the nature of existing institutions and by the relation of individuals to these institutions. An individual may change his relation to an institutional complex. He may go to a university. Universities are much more open than they were fifty or a hundred years ago. He may change his relation to economic institutions through trade-union processes or through the nationalization of industry. The class structure, in this sense, is not modified by persons moving from one class to another; but rather people move as a result of change in the institutional arrangements.

Cole is not concerned with the possible loss of a middle-class style of life because it rests upon a set of values which are unacceptable to him, or at least cannot be demonstrated to be superior to the values basic to a working-class way of life. Certainly these middle-class values cannot compete with the set of values supporting the concept of a classless society.

Thus it is demonstrated again that one's analysis of the social structure is dependent upon the concepts employed and, in addition, is likely to be influenced by ideologies held.

chapter eight

SOCIALIZATION OF THE PROFESSIONS*

This brief discussion will attempt to analyze certain problems associated with the socialization (or nationalization) of the professions. Portions of British experience will be drawn upon by way of illustration. It is maintained that the differences between the professions and other vocations are such as to raise problems which are of a special character in relation to socialization. In the case of business and industry, nationalization results in a logically consistent condition of unified ownership, management, and control. The socialization of a *profession* does not involve ownership per se, but raises problems of management, and necessitates divided control. The problem is essentially one of *relationship between knowledge and authority.*

The professions are marked off from other common occupational pursuits by certain peculiar characteristics: (1) an intellectual basis for practicing a specialized art; (2) a relationship between practitioner and client which involves trust and acceptance of authority on the part of the client; (3) the role of the professional association as it functions in relation to members of the profession and as a source of authority in forming public policy; (4) the existence of professional codes of ethics dedicating the practitioner to his art and the public good; and (5) in relation to the code of professional ethics, the disavowal of personal pecuniary motives and the avoidance of commercialism.[42] Carr-Saunders and Wilson say, near the end of their study, after originally declining to offer a definition on the assumption that everyone recognizes professions as a result of their traditional

---

* Presented at the American Sociological Association meetings, Chicago, 1959.

status: "We have found that the application of an intellectual
technique to the ordinary business of life, acquired as the result
of prolonged and specialized training, is the chief distinguishing
characteristic of the professions."[43] The essentially intellectual
basis of the professions is commonly agreed upon. The technique
or art which is employed is built upon a body of specialized
knowledge acquired by following a prescribed advanced course
of study. The professional's mastery of a specialized segment of
knowledge is such as to engender trust in his client, and indeed
it is thought to be the highest source of authority in respect to
the practice of the technique.

The importance of the professional organization centers around
the relationship of practitioners to the association and the relation
of the association to the public. These associations guarantee the
technical efficiency of their members by indirectly controlling
training, by certification, and by supervision of functioning. The
associations also impose the code of ethics which includes, in
general terms, the duty to offer service whenever and wherever
it is required, to maintain high standards, and to abstain from
competition and other behavior associated with commercializa-
tion. The professional is first dedicated to his art—making a living
is incidental. Such ethical codes are based upon the belief that
between professional and client there is a relationship of trust,
whereas, between buyer and seller there is not. The professional
must be trusted to give what he cannot be compelled or con-
tractually bound to give.[44] The professional association also has
the function of maintaining an implied contract with society to
provide the best possible service within the existing state of
knowledge. Professional service by its very nature is not standardized, but at the same time it is essentially impersonal in that
the primary function is in practicing the art in accordance with
known principles, irrespective of personality, ethnicity, race,
status, or class position of the client.[45] Another function of the
professional association is to protect the particular field against
invasion by unqualified persons and to be concerned with such
matters as proper modes of payment for services and to quietly
determine standards of remuneration. The professional association, in the private organization and functioning of the profession,

represents the seat of both knowledge and authority. With the advent of socialization, the responsibilities and functions of professional associations are of necessity modified. Change is not easily brought about, as each association has a long history of development culminating in its present structure and operation.

A consideration of the historical background of the relationship between the state and professional associations would indicate that the socialization of the professions in England since World War II has raised no essentially new problems. Only education, social work, and medicine have been socialized* and in each of these professions there remain wide areas of private practice. Medicine is the most completely socialized, with only 1 or 2 percent of the doctors remaining entirely outside of the National Health Service.

With the socialization of these professions, the relationship of professional associations to the state has come to be advisory rather than determining in regard to matters of public policy; they remain authoritative in all technical knowledge, professional ethics, and in general supervision of practice. Carr-Saunders and Wilson pointed out over twenty-five years ago: "Professional associations are not the only repositories of knowledge, but they are the repositories of a very special kind of knowledge. . . ."[46] It would seem that this observation has been kept in mind during the process of socialization.

At this point we will utilize the socialization of the medical profession in Britain to analyze changes, or the lack of changes, in relation to the peculiar characteristics of the professions.

In the last half of the nineteenth century, Britain established a comprehensive public health service concerned largely with research, sanitation, and general preventative medicine. This program preceded the development of personal health services. The National Insurance Act of 1911 was the first step in the provision of the state-aided general practitioner, that is, outside the long-established Poor Law provisions.[47]

Long before the National Health Service (NHS) came into effect in July, 1948, more than half of the patients of English

---

* I omit the professional Civil Service and the military.

doctors were "panel" patients under the provisions of the National Insurance Act. Ninety percent of the doctors chose to participate in the NHS at the time of its instigation, and at the present time ninety-nine percent are practicing within the NHS, at least part of the time. Ninety-seven percent of the population have their names on the NHS doctors' roles.[48]

In this comprehensive system,[49] what has occurred in relation to our concept of professionalism? As has been indicated previously, in socialization, the professional association must relinquish some power and authority. In the case of the NHS, the Minister of Health has the ultimate control. He is responsible to Parliament and thus to the people. However, the NHS Act created an advisory body—the Central Health Services Council—to advise the Minister on professional and technical questions. This forty-one-member council is composed of members of the medical profession, kindred professions, and others with special qualifications in hospital management and local government. The president of the Royal College of Surgeons and certain other officials of established professional associations are automatically included in the Council and the other members are appointed by the Minister after consultation with the relevant professional associations. The Council's function is purely advisory and the Minister is not bound to take its advice, but he is required by the Act to bring its annual report before Parliament and in this way the views of the Council are made public. In addition to the advisory council there are nine advisory standing committees on nine areas of special medical problems.*

The Minister of Health may dismiss a doctor from the service. However, an appeal tribunal exists and the Minister cannot reverse its decision except in favor of the doctor. The doctor's contract of employment is with the local hospital board or the executive council rather than with the Ministry of Health. He is thus not directly what we would term a "federal employee." The Minister cannot compel a practitioner to accept a particular patient on his list, nor can he compel a particular patient to avail

---

* Medical, dental, pharmaceutical, opthalmic, nursing, maternity, mental health, tuberculosis, cancer, and radiotherapy.

himself of the services of a certain doctor. The general practitioner is remunerated by capitation fees based upon the number of persons on his list.

This mode of payment is important in maintaining appropriate doctor-patient relationships. The doctor's relationship with patients remains unchanged; his personal and professional success is dependent, in large part, upon maintaining good professional relationships with patients.

These are enough of the details of the organization to indicate the modification of function of the professional association and the existing relationship between knowledge and authority under socialization. It is obvious that the profession relinquishes a certain amount of authority to essentially political agencies. However, the profession is represented in these agencies and the weight of its knowledge continues to be felt.

One aspect of professionalism remains to be discussed in relation to the NHS—that of financial remuneration. As we pointed out previously, the professional's first obligation is to his art and society; all pecuniary interest, commercialism, and the market mentality must, according to the mores of the group, be shunned. We maintain that socialization of the medical profession offers a powerful assist to the physican in complying with these laudable professional expectations. The doctors' situation in Britain will illustrate this important point.

First, under the NHS method of payment, as mentioned above, no money passes between doctor and patient. Instead, the state, in recognition of his service to society[50] sends him a check through impersonal bureaucratic channels. The doctor is thus relieved of the non-professional, status-damaging commercial activities of keeping accounts, sending requests for payment, fraternizing with credit bureaus and collection agencies.

Despite this outward disdain for the market, professional people are not only interested in "making a living" but also in maintaining a certain style of life thought to be necessary and proper in relation to their position as professionals. In the British situation there was much study and discussion preceding the determination of levels of remuneration.[51] As to prevailing levels of pay, it should be pointed out that the general practitioner, having an average number of people on his roles, receives approximately 2,370 pounds a year ($6,636)[52] and that less than 1 percent of employed persons in England receive over 2,000 pounds a year.[53] A general practitioner having a maximum number of patients on his roles, has an income of approximately 3,475 pounds ($10,000) a year.*

"The starting salaries in many professional and technical careers are often in the range of 350 to 500 pounds a year. Most of the senior posts in business, the professions and the Civil Service are in the range from 1,000 to 5,000 pounds a year."[54] Thus, the doctors' financial status compares very favorably with other professions in Britain and is, indeed, at the very top level of income receivers in the country.

The peculiar nature of the professions as we have seen, raises certain problems in relation to socialization. The most serious of these center about the transference of a certain amount of traditional, almost monopolistic power and authority from professional associations to the state. The change has not been of a sudden nature. Socialization may be seen as merely the logical end of a process of expanding state responsibility for the public welfare. T. H. Marshall says, "There has been a silent revolution in the social services to which the professions are adapting themselves. It is not a painful process, because the adaptation does not involve a surrender of any of the fundamentals of the professional ideal."[55] One of the peculiar aspects of the professions is that they have always been more *social* than other vocations. Marshall summarizes the contemporary situation as follows:

> Admittedly the situation is dangerous when a free profession must work under the orders of a superior. The commands of the superior may clash with the conscience of the profession, and this is particularly serious when the commands are backed by the unlimited power of the State. But I believe that in modern democratic societies this danger is diminishing rather than increasing, because the State and professions are being assimilated to one another. This is not happening through the absorption of the profession by the State but by both of them moving from

---

* See "Socialized Medicine," *infra*, for 1962 estimates of doctors' incomes and discussion.

opposite directions to meet in the middle position. The natural foe of professionalism in private life is commercialism. Its natural foe in public life is politics, in the less respectable sense of that term. Both bring extraneous motives and scales of value inappropriate to the real business at hand.[56]

It may be that the "assimilation" of the state and the professions, of which Marshall speaks, will be facilitated by the large-scale trend of change in concepts of government responsibility in a democratic society. As social services are expanded and appropriate bureaucracies are developed for their administration, power and authority of the more political will be transferred to the more professional in the offices of a growing corps of technical advisors and administrators who are themselves socialized professionals.

chapter nine

CHANGES IN CLASS AND STATUS OF OCCUPATIONAL GROUPS IN AN ENGLISH TOWN*

England, as is well known, is a highly industrialized country. Numerous small towns and villages, however, have remained primarily rural. During and after World War II, industries were located in or near many of these towns, one of which is Tewkesbury, Gloucestershire, located at the confluence of the Severn and Avon rivers. The physical appearance of Tewkesbury is much the same today as it was in medieval times. It is dominated by the Abbey—a beautiful Norman structure which stands as a reminder of nine hundred years of history. The buildings of the town consist of a haphazard assortment of ancient half-timbered houses and shops with Georgian buildings among them. Narrow alleys lead from the main street into courts of crowded "cottages." These are the slums of Tewkesbury. The buildings are old and dilapidated. Some are still without running water. Despite the flower boxes and whitewash they provide the lowest level of human shelter. As is indicated later, many of these old houses have been condemned and razed, but a large number of people are still living, as did their forefathers for many generations, in the alleys of Tewkesbury.[57]

The town has long served as a farm market center. In the past, the only industries were milling, boatbuilding on a small scale, and weaving by the "putting out" system. Many of the people have made their living for many generations by seasonal farm work and by what they could get from the rivers by fishing,

---

* From *Research Studies,* Washington State University, Vol. XXVII, No. 2, 1959.

cutting osiers, dredging sand, setting traps for eels, and poaching from more serious fishermen. From descriptions of Tewkesbury in preindustrial times, it would seem that when there was no farm work to be done, many of the men were technically unemployed. At these times, they were able to gain a meager living by exploiting the rivers and by doing odd jobs and carrying on small domestic enterprises such as raising rabbits, catching and breeding goldfinches, or making trinkets and furniture.

With my family, I lived in Tewkesbury (actually just over the county line in Worcestershire) for seven months in the spring and summer of 1957. In addition to the experience of day-to-day living in the community, I carried on a systematic program of participant observation. In the course of this work I became acquainted with many individuals and families. Informal interviews were conducted, and I responded to invitations to participate in meetings of school and civic organizations. Interviews with several older residents of the community were especially fruitful and augmented historical information obtained from town records. Information secured in this fashion was supplemented by the use of a paper-and-pencil ranking questionnaire which is described later.

The purpose of this study is to determine what changes took place in the social evaluation of occupations following the coming of industry to this small English market town. In order to see these changes in proper perspective, I shall first make some observations upon broader aspects of changes in the community resulting from recent industrialization.

Existing records show that the population of Tewkesbury reached a peak of 6,000 in the middle of the nineteenth century. Later, the main line of the railway bypassed the town. Much of the traffic which the rivers had previously carried now went by rail. In the 1920's, the town, being effectively isolated from the mainstream of commerce and industry, depended almost entirely upon buying and selling farm produce. With a general recession in agriculture, intensified by the foot-and-mouth disease, Tewkesbury became a quiet, stagnating town which steadily lost population through the 1930's, until in 1939 it had reached a low of 4,345. In that year the first of two new industries, a large plant manufacturing hydraulic machinery and airplane parts, was established. At about the same time, a nearby clock factory was enlarged and converted to manufacturing precision instruments. During the war, a military vehicle base was situated in the town. The military base was retained after the war, and the two manufacturing plants were greatly expanded. After 1939, the population rose steadily: in 1947 to 4,728; in 1951 to 5,233; in 1955 to 6,179.[58]

The first result of industrialization was thus to reverse the downward trend in population. As the population steadily increased from 1939 onward, the old houses which composed the "slums" of Tewkesbury's alleys, the old row houses which had been built back of the main streets hundreds of years ago, became more and more overcrowded, and undesirable living conditions worsened. The Town Council and the County Planning Authority took steps to relieve the intolerable situation. Many houses were condemned and razed. Two new housing estates (projects) were built adjacent to the old town. These new houses were occupied by persons forced to move from the slums and by a new population which was drawn into the community by the growing industry. The public-housing areas, with their uniform, dull brick multiple houses, standing uncrowded along well laid out streets, presented a striking contrast to the cluttered "higgledy-piggledy" appearance of the ancient town. The influence of industrialization was gradually changing the appearance of Tewkesbury. In 1957 approximately 3,000, or half the population, lived in the Prior's Park housing estate.

The labor force is not only growing, but is being employed in radically different ways than in earlier times. The table shows in percentages the extreme changes in distribution of the labor force between 1939 and 1956: While agricultural labor was dropping from more than a third to about one-twelfth of the total, industrial labor swelled from about one-seventh to more than half. In services, the changes were less spectacular, rising from less than one-half to just over one-half and then dropping off in 1956 to slightly over one-third; but within that category (not analyzed in the table), the percentage engaged in professional services increased from 1.4 to 5.0; service work connected with gas, water,

TABLE 1—*Distribution of the Working Force, Tewkesbury*

Industry	1939*	1948*	1956†
Manufacturing	14.0%	21.6%	52.9%
Agriculture	37.4	23.4	8.5
Services	48.6	54.7	38.5
Total:	100.0	99.7	99.9

* Approximation.
† *Tewkesbury—Draft Analysis*, Gloucestershire Town and Country Planning
Authority (mimeographed), 1957, p. 8.

and electricity almost doubled; public administration, insurance
and banking, and distributive trades remained about the same.
The service occupations which experienced the greatest decline
were domestic and other personal services. The working force
totalled 5,468 (male and female), including 1,800 workers who
lived outside of the community and were brought in to work
daily by private bus.[59]

The reaction of the old inhabitants to these changes was
divided. Most of them—the shopkeepers, bankers, insurance men,
restaurant owners and publicans—were happy with the new
conditions. The increased population meant expanded purchasing
power and a generally higher level of business. Their only com-
plaints seemed to be that they could not compete with "the
factory" for labor. Sales clerks and domestic servants were difficult to locate and employ at wages lower than those paid to
factory workers. School men accepted the changes as desirable.
Several older teachers thought that the "infusion of new blood"
into the community was quite beneficial. They said that there
had been much intermarriage among the "lower classes" for
many generations, and that a dull or moronic group of some size
was being perpetuated. Whether or not this was true I was
unable to determine, though similar comments were made by
other informants.

A sizable group of old residents, however, resented the changes.
Some of the old established leaders in the community, land-

owners and *rentiers*, preferred the old regime. They disliked the "kind of people" who were moving in—working class from larger cities. They pointed to new milk bars with their counter stools, dirty tables, juke boxes, and Coca-Cola. The children of the new working class didn't show proper respect, and there was some question about the behavior of young people. An old Tudor pub on the edge of town had been expanded into an adjoining barn and made into a dance hall. It was patronized exclusively by working-class people, and on Saturday nights it presented a disorderly, rowdy scene.

With the new industry, the new population, and the new economic prosperity, it was evident that a shift was also taking place in the power relations. The local squire had lost his traditional influence some time ago; the old manor house was now a public home for the aged. Prominent landowners had, however, retained their power until the period just before World War II. Businessmen now occupy influential offices. The election of one (middle-class) member of the Labour Party to the City Council gave evidence of the growing strength of the new working-class population. The "old guard" recognize these changes as hastening their own decline.

As an approach to the problem of changes in social evaluation of occupational groups, I used a ranking device which was completed by twenty informants. All the informants selected were long-time residents in the community, who appeared to know it well and also to understand the project on which I was working. The group included persons from the major social classes in the community, but could not be considered representative. The ranking instrument contained two pages. On each page, fifteen occupational groups were listed under two time periods—1918 to 1938, and 1939 to the present. Each list was accompanied by a diagram showing six class levels of equal proportions. On the first page the criterion of social class position was stated as prestige and influence; on the second page the criterion of social class was income and economic well-being. Otherwise the pages were identical. The respondents were asked to indicate by each criterion the class position of each occupational group in the respective time periods. The six hypothetical classes in the diagram were designated upper upper, lower upper, upper middle, lower middle, upper working, and lower working. The informants thus functioned as judges rather than as any form of sample. Changes in the class position of ten of the occupations are discussed here, and the most significant changes in social class position since 1939, as perceived by these informants in relation to each criterion, are summarized. These ten are selected because they include occupations in which various amounts of change occurred between the two time periods. In the case of headmasters (of schools), owners and managers of factories, domestic servants, farm laborers, and small farm freeholders, there had been relatively little change, except among small farm freeholders. In their case the raters indicated that recent financial gains had brought their economic position up to the traditional middle-class social status.[60]

The changes in social class position indicated by the twenty judges are briefly reported below. These differences represent changes in the social evaluation of the occupational groups occurring after 1939, that is, after the coming of industry to the community.

1. The data from the ranking questionnaire relative to factory workers, using income and economic well-being as a criterion of social class, reveal a significant economic gain in the period after 1939. All twenty informants indicated upward mobility of from one to three classes. The movements were from either the lower working class in the first period, to the lower middle class, or from the upper working class to the lower middle and upper middle class. Using prestige as a criterion of social class, fifteen of twenty informants showed a rise of one or more classes, most commonly from lower working to upper working. Thus, in general terms, the prestige of factory workers lagged behind their economic gains.

2. There has been relatively little change in the class position of small shopkeepers. Most informants placed them in the lower middle class by each criterion in each time period.

3. Clergymen retained their traditional high prestige, but their money income during the second period declined markedly. Most informants placed the clergy, on the basis of prestige, in the

upper upper, lower upper, and upper middle classes. On the economic side, the informants indicated a decrease in class status in the second period of from two to three classes; economically, the clergy was almost uniformly considered to be upper working class.

4. The prestige of doctors remained high—upper middle to upper upper—and, on the economic side, nearly half of the informants indicated a rise of one class in the later time period, placing them in the upper middle to upper upper class.

5. As to school teachers, there was relatively little consistency in the responses. Most of the informants thought that school teachers were lower middle class by both criteria and in both time periods. However, nearly half of the rankers indicated that teachers lost class position on the economic side.

6. Unskilled and casual workers had not gained in prestige, but their income position was improved over the earlier period. Over half of the informants indicated at least one class rise, from lower working to upper working, on the basis of the economic criterion.

7. As to clerks (not salespeople, but white-collar clerical workers, usually in banks and other financial institutions) the data were confused. Almost all informants thought that clerks had changed their class status between the two periods. Most informants indicated a drop in prestige from upper middle to lower middle or upper working class, but some indicated a one-class upward movement. On the economic side, there was somewhat more consistency in showing a lower original class status, upper working or lower working, and a movement to one class higher in the later time period.

8. In regard to bankers, the responses from the questionnaires were quite uniform, indicating practically no change between time periods, their class status on both criteria being fairly evenly distributed between upper upper, lower upper, and upper middle.

9. Artisans shared in the general upward mobility of the working class in the second time period. The data revealed a rise, both on the basis of prestige and economically. The economic gain almost uniformly took artisans out of the upper working class into the lower middle and upper middle classes. The rise in prestige was not uniform.

10. Large farm estate holders maintained high prestige. The questionnaire data were fairly evenly divided, placing large landowners in either the upper upper or upper middle prestige class, and showing little change between time periods. On the economic side, the questionnaire data were not consistent. About half of the respondents indicated a movement upward in the class structure. Others indicated no change or a downward movement.

Probably the most interesting revelation of these data is that, on the basis of income and economic well-being—but not in prestige—both factory workers and artisans are now considered to be middle-class. This may explain the resentment shown by many of the old middle class toward the changes which accompanied industrialization in the community.

The changes revealed in the social evaluation of occupations cannot, of course, be exclusively related to the effects of industrialization in the local community. They are, rather, a single instance in a process of change which has similarly affected many other small towns in England since World War II,[61] and the economic gains of traditional working-class occupations as revealed here coincide with a similar upward movement in urban areas.[62]

In the investigation of general social changes in Tewkesbury, I was frequently told that "there is no longer a working class in England." This kind of statement, made with only the criterion of economic well-being in mind, was borne out by data obtained from the ranking questionnaire. The remaining low *social* status and prestige of the working class presents a problem to which much attention is being given in England at present.[63]

In this particular town—Tewkesbury—ecological and demographic changes are evident. The spatial distribution of residents is altered; the size and nature of the population is changed; the distribution of the labor force is drastically different from that before industrialization; the class structure has been modified both in the social evaluation of occupational groups and in power relations in the community.

In Tewkesbury, however, it should be pointed out that the new and the old are conspicuously coexistent; innovation and tradition, as in all England, go hand in hand.

chapter ten

SOCIAL CLASS AND STATUS OF THE SMALL FREEHOLDER IN THE ENGLISH MIDLANDS*

Social class relationships have undergone considerable change in England since World War II. Much attention has been given to changes in economic well-being and social status in urban populations where the widespread gains of the working class are most obvious.[64] Less is known about recent changes in rural areas.

The method employed in this study was, first, participant observation while my family and I lived in a rural community in Worcestershire, England. We shared an old Tudor farmhouse with a small farm freeholder for seven months. The second source of data was in the use of a pencil and paper rating device.

One accustomed to the life and manners of the Midlands can identify a small freeholder by sight. His customary garb—his working and marketing clothes—are as distinctive in the country as are the bowler hat, black coat, and stiff collar of the clerks in the city. The small farmer traditionally wears a colored dress shirt, detachable collar, tie, wool trousers stuffed into the tops of rubber boots, and a felt hat which has seen better days. While working about the farm, he wears a khaki smock which may be replaced by a short coat on market days. This garb identifies him, not only as a farmer, but also as a gentleman. In relation to the great Victorian dichotomy of English society—gentlemen and others—the small farmer is definitely in the preferred category.

I was interested in translating this traditional status into con-

---

* From *Rural Sociology*, Vol. XXIII, No. 4, 1958.

temporary social class terms. My observations were guided by criteria which have frequently been used in the process of social evaluation in relation to stratificational position, i.e., property ownership, type of residence, education, and style of life, including informal associations.

Small freeholders in this section of England commonly own from a few acres to possibly thirty or forty acres of land. Milk cows, swine, and chickens are the source of most of their produce. A few farmers have developed rather large garden plots. The ownership of farm land has been the basis of their status as gentlemen and continues to be an important factor determining their contemporary position in society.

The most common type of small farm residence in this area is an old brick or half-timbered house which was originally built sometime between the sixteenth and eighteenth centuries. The Tudor houses consisted originally of a relatively large hall downstairs with a fireplace across one end and two or three bedrooms upstairs. These buildings have had kitchens and frequently other rooms added in later times. Most of the houses are now connected with county water and sewage lines (the house we lived in was not), and all have electricity. This does not mean that they are "modern." Heating is frequently by open fire in each room, and kitchens and bathrooms have an antiquated makeshift appearance. They do not compare favorably with middle-class homes in the towns and cities and are indeed primitive when compared with the new working-class public housing.* However, many of the farmhouses lend their occupants high prestige, because they are "period" houses set in attractive grounds, and kept in good repair.

Thus, when these houses are assessed upon a contemporary scale of living comforts, they are certainly near the bottom.

---

* The small farmers resented the rather recent building of a small public housing project in the community. They all feared that another such project would be built near their property. Their objections were ostensibly on aesthetic grounds. However, the public housing was occupied exclusively by working-class families, and there was reason to believe that the farmers' objections were expressions of class prejudices—or possibly more accurately, of snobbery.

Nevertheless, they are high-status houses and are considered so by both their occupants and others in the community.

Formal education is difficult to assess. However, language is frequently an indicator of status and class[65] and is often related to the type of school the person has attended. The small farmer speaks the dialect of the particular region. It is not the language of the grammar-school or college graduate, nor is it the vernacular of the farm laborer or town worker. One may say that the small farmer speaks correctly the traditional language of the area. In terms of social status, he is thus set off from both the working and the educated classes.

The small farm freeholder has a distinctive way of life. He makes his living by manual labor and at the same time tries to live like a gentleman. He is condescending to day-laborers and feels out of place with both the urban working and middle classes. He shows deference to the remaining squires and large estate holders, but I think he may picture himself as a smaller version of the same.

There is a rather clearer class division in the community between the farmers on the one hand and the farm laborers and other working-class people on the other. The local Spring Fête was organized and presented with very little working-class support or participation. The class division is also illustrated by informal association at two rural pubs in the area. One of the pubs was entirely working-class, having no "lounge bar." The other pub had the usual class-typed dual facilities. The farmers patronized the "lounge bar" of the second pub almost exclusively. I observed no association, either formal or informal, which could possibly be interpreted as an expression of social equality.

The foregoing descriptive impressions are based upon what I could learn through both impromptu and prearranged interviews and upon a knowledge of the community which was acquired through associations made by participating in organized and informal community activities. Schools, doctors, hospital, pubs, and horse races, community fêtes, children's play groups, visiting, and gossip, not to mention the daily round of shopping, all contributed to insights into and to at least a limited understanding of these rural people.

The second approach to the problem was the use of an occupational ranking device.* This was a two-page questionnaire listing the same fifteen occupations on each page, under two time periods—1918 to 1939 and 1939 to the present. Accompanying each list was a diagram showing six class levels of equal size. The levels were designated "upper upper," "lower upper," "upper middle," "lower middle," "upper working," and "lower working." On the first page the respondent was asked to designate the class level he thought proper of each occupational group in each time period *using prestige and influence in the community as the criteria of placement.* On the second page the procedure was the same except that the criteria of placement were *income and economic well-being.* The twenty respondents did not form a sample of any kind, but rather functioned as judges. The factors taken into consideration in the selection of these judges were length of residence in the community, their knowledge of the community, and their understanding of the project. The respondents were selected from both the farming area and the small town which was the market center of the community. Although among them were persons of widely varying social status, no judge was selected from the group of small farm freeholders.

The data from these rankings indicated that nearly all of the respondents considered small farm freeholders either lower-middle or upper-middle class on the basis of prestige and further showed but little change between time periods. However, upon the basis of income and economic well-being, the respondents indicated upper-working-class status in the first period (1918-39) and lower-middle- or upper-middle-class position at the present time. Thus, these data revealed that recent improvements in economic well-being had brought the small farmer up to his traditional middle-class prestige level.

This is interesting when compared with changes in social class status or other occupational groups in the community.[66] For example, in relation to large farm estate holders, although most rankers showed status continuing in the upper-middle or

---

* This is the same technique as that described in the previous study. It utilizes the distinction between status and class.

upper social class on the basis of each criterion, there was some evidence of downward mobility in both status and economic well-being. Farm laborers, on the other hand, had moved up from the lower working class to the upper working class both economically and in prestige.

The case of the small farm freeholder was unique in that his previously established middle-class prestige not only has been maintained but has recently been vindicated by economic gains.

chapter eleven

BUREAUCRACY AND BRITISH
SOCIALISM*

Bureaucracy, in its literal meaning, refers to rule or control through a system of offices or bureaus. The organizational structure is hierarchal in nature, which means that there are several levels of offices in a system of superordination and subordination. In the fully developed bureaucracy, the office hierarchy is monocratically organized—authority comes down from the top, and below the policy-making level the office tends to assume more importance than its incumbent.[67]

The function of a bureaucracy is to control, manage, or order administrative regulations or laws in accordance with strict rules and within well-defined jurisdictional areas. The execution of such regulations is carried out in an impersonal and impartial manner by bureaucrats who have special training and experience and are selected for their posts either by special examination or by appointment.[68]

Bureaucratic organization is found not only in political and economic areas but also in religious, fraternal, and other types of groups demanding large-scale administration. It is frequently associated with bigness. However, it should not be considered synonymous with "large organization."[69]

Bureaucracy should be defined in terms of structure and function rather than in terms of size. Also, for purposes of definition, whether or not the organization is private or public is irrelevant.

The process of bureaucratization in England is associated on the economic side with the development of capitalism and the ac-

---

* From *Sociology and Social Research,* Vol. XXXVII, No. 3, 1953.

companying process of rationalization. Politically, it is associated first with the rule of the aristocracy and second with nineteenth-century liberalism and the political power of the upper middle classes.[70]

An increase in the amount of bureaucracy has been associated with state ownership. In this process, however, the number of bureaucrats could have either decreased or increased, but it does not necessarily change as the result of nationalization per se. With the nationalization of an existing industry, administrative authority shifts from private enterprise to public control. Thus the number of bureaucrats employed directly or indirectly by the *state* necessarily increases,[71] but this number may be no greater than the number previously engaged in the private organization.

The real cause of the increased bureaucratization in England under the Labour government was the *expanded function* of government in this process, and in the creation of bureaucratic structures to regulate the administration of *new* services. No doubt, everywhere that the function of the state has expanded, government bureaucracy has grown in size and power, but its importance should not be exaggerated by ascribing to it effects of which it is not a cause.[72] Hyneman, writing about the United States, points out that the increased size of bureaucracy is the result of existing government policy, not the product of mere administrative inefficiency. "It must be understood that the size of a federal bureaucracy is far less affected by the quality of administrative management . . . than it is by the scope of activity which the administrative branch of the government has to carry out."[73]

The real problem is then: Are there too few or too many bureaucrats, in the light of the degree of control intended and desired? The Labour government in England extended control. Socialist measures consisted of three kinds: the extension of social services such as health and education, the nationalization of certain sectors of the national economy, and the regulation and control of those sectors which remained in private hands.

A difference of opinion exists, however, as to the "degree of control intended and desired" in these areas. The steady increase in the popular vote supporting the Labour Party from 1945 to

1951 and the tacit acceptance of the principal aspects of the welfare state by the Conservative party indicate that greatly increased state planning and control are very widely supported by the English people. Furthermore, this quasi-socialist revolution has its roots far back in English history and is considered to be little more than the development of the principles of "positive liberalism." In other words, these changes represent no sharp break in principle, as shown both by history and by the strict constitutionality which characterized the method of their initiation. Although these developments in themselves are considered to be an extension of democracy, the bureaucratic structures which are associated with their implementation have given rise to serious problems.

The first of these structures, the permanent civil service, fashioned by Northcote and Trevelyan and by a long line of middle-class administrators, was a most adequate instrument for the laissez-faire state. Its structure and function were primarily the result of the demands put upon it by the upper middle classes, and those classes neither asked for nor expected great things of the state. They were content with a governmental mechanism which would insure their property and investments, and which would continue their position of social and economic power at home and abroad.[74] The notable impartiality of the British Civil Service[75] was not too difficult to maintain for a period of approximately seventy-five years, inasmuch as the bureaucrats in the policy-making grades saw eye to eye on fundamentals with the dominant power group in the society—the middle classes. The civil service during this period was what Kingsley calls a "representative bureaucracy."

Now that a rather definite shift in power relations has occurred[76] in favor of the working class, the middle-class civil service is no longer as "representative" as it was previously, and it is therefore less responsive. Labour ministers did not bring about a drastic change in the bureaucratic function of their various departments. In fact, in a bureaucratically organized activity, the existing structure and personnel tend to operate in such a manner as to hinder social reform.[77] Thus, as policy of the Labour government was implemented, the regular civil service became less and less representative. This unrepresentativeness of the civil service (although important changes have been made) presented a problem to the Labour government.

This problem may be partially solved through education. The British Civil Service has always been very closely coordinated with the educational system. That is, certain grades have always been open only to candidates who have completed designated educational units in specific types of schools and are within a limited age range. The 1944 Education Act for the first time provided secondary education for all children at public expense, and otherwise went a long way in democratizing education. In time, by breaking down the highly class-biased school system, this in itself will broaden the basis of recruitment to the civil service. Thus, it is reasonable to believe that as the effects of the new school system are felt in the society and as the shift in power relations becomes more pronounced, the civil service will gradually become representative of the new power situation.

A somewhat different problem was encountered by the Labour government in developing bureaucratic structures for the operation of nationalized industries. These new Public Boards control the Bank of England, civil aviation, coal, electricity and gas, cotton (raw buying), transport (except trucking), and medicine. In these Public Boards, authority is vested in the Cabinet Minister, and he has more control over these boards than was usually true in the old, established bureaucracies of the civil service. This is true for several reasons: first, they are new and lack the tradition of the civil service; second, all members are appointed; third, they tend to be highly centralized;[78] fourth, centralized authority was thought to be necessary in order to coordinate economic planning. In addition to the above, the new boards are less financially independent, and their members may be dismissed by the Minister as being "unfit to continue in office."[79]

Non-socialists were sometimes appointed as members of the New National Boards because of a shortage of highly trained administrators and technicians. This situation caused some difficulty under the Labour government, but the amount of sabotage resulting from such appointments has probably been exaggerated.

If such men did not cooperate, they were seldom indispensable.*

The appointment of personnel to these new boards, at all levels, has departed without notable advantage from the established criteria of civil service.[80] The degree of centralization of power in reference to some of the boards has removed authority too far from the field of action and has raised problems of intercommunication between the government and the governed. The Conservatives have tried to remedy these difficulties by various measures of reorganization—not by abolishment.

One other problem of a more subjective nature, but no less real, is the relation of bureaucracy to socialist theory.[81] The Labour movement, and socialists generally, believed that, with the coming of socialism, the common man would enjoy greater participation in government—"A rubbing out of the dividing line between government and governed; between 'us' and 'them'." The expanded *governmental* bureaucracy which was necessary to convert socialist theory into social policy made the line between government and the governed, if not more real, at least more obvious than it had been before. The gulf which had existed between the worker and the big boss was now frequently found between the worker and the bureaucrat. The gulf is no larger than before. In fact, it is probably less distinct, as is revealed by a comparison of labor-management relations following World War I with conditions during the recent past.† People, generally speaking, are not disappointed by the accomplishments of the Labour government nor in the way the program has been carried out by Conservative governments since 1951. (Nationalization was not a major issue in the recent election.) The disappointment, where it exists, is associated with the disparity between the expectation of a political and social transformation, which had been pictured by socialist writings, and the actual socio-political situation. This condition has given rise in many to a sense of remoteness in relation to the expanded bureaucratic governmental structure.

---

* R. H. Tawney, in conversation with the writer, expressed this same thought: "We are not that short of good men."

† The two periods are hardly comparable, as the period following World War I was characterized by widespread unemployment.

The present period of transition in England has exaggerated the so-called "democracy-bureaucracy dilemma."[82] It seems reasonable, however, to postulate that as equal opportunity for education and the new class and power relations are further realized throughout the society, the new bureaucracy will become as well adapted, as representative, and as well accepted as was the old civil service in the laissez-faire state of the nineteenth century. When this is accomplished, the disparity between socialist theory and bureaucracy and the resulting feeling of remoteness from government will no longer exist among the masses of people.

chapter twelve

THE WELFARE STATE AND SOCIAL
CLASS—SOCIALIZED MEDICINE
AND EDUCATION

A welfare state is merely a state which has assumed the responsibility for securing the general welfare of its citizens, and has not only proclaimed this to be a proper function of the state, but has established the governmental machinery necessary to administer such services as are necessary and has indicated that they are willing to pay for it out of the national budget. "It guarantees a minimum of subsistence without removing incentives to personal enterprise, and it brings about a limited redistribution of income by means of graduated high taxation, yet does not pretend to establish economic equality among its citizens. All are assured of adequate help in case of need, whether the need is due to illness, old age, unemployment or any other cause."[83] In the English welfare state, assistance is considered to be a right, not a matter of charity, and is given without any stigma of pauperism.

The welfare state in England is not particularly new—parts of it are of recent development but it has a long history which we cannot trace at this time. Suffice it to say here that such histories usually begin with the Elizabethan Poor Law of 1601. However, even Henry VIII, who is not usually thought of either as a "do-gooder" or as an "egghead," after the dissolution of the monasteries, supported the law requiring "the regular collection and distribution of alms." Disraeli, who has been called the grandfather of the welfare state, was keenly aware of class differences. He described England as two nations. In a mid-nineteenth century novel, he wrote of them as: "Two nations between whom there is no intercourse, and no sympathy, who are as ignorant of each other's habits, thoughts, and feelings, as if they were dwellers in different zones, or inhabitants of different planets; who are formed by different breedings, are fed by a different food, are ordered by different manners, and are not governed by the same laws. . . . The rich and the poor." As Prime Minister during the 1870's, Disraeli fostered significant welfare legislation.

If Disraeli was the grandfather of the welfare state, Lord Beveridge was the father. It is important to remember that the Beveridge Report (the report of a Parliamentary committee) was accepted by the Coalition Government of Winston Churchill. All three political parties, Conservative, Liberal, and Labour agreed in their intention to make this great experiment in an effort to overcome poverty and to create the welfare state. Under the Labour government of 1945-51, legislation implementing the Beveridge Report was passed.

Socialized Medicine

The British do not use the term "socialized medicine"; however, the National Health Service Act of 1946 made all health care a public function. The expressed aim of the Act was "the establishment in England and Wales of a comprehensive health service designed to secure improvement in physical and mental health of the people . . . the prevention, diagnosis and treatment of illness without regard to the patients' ability to pay."[84] Through the provisions of this Act the Minister of Health was made responsible to Parliament for seeing "that health services of every kind and of the highest possible quality, were available to everyone who needed them."[85]

On July 5th, 1948, the National Health Service (NHS) began to function throughout England and Wales. Scotland established a similar program at about the same time. The NHS is made up of three main parts: the general practitioner (family doctor) and dental services, the hospital and specialist services, and the local health authority functions.

Ninety per cent of the general practitioners chose to participate in the NHS in 1948 and now all but 2 per cent are practicing in the service. The great majority of specialists are practicing within the NHS, and nearly all the dentists and pharmacists are taking part.

At the beginning of the NHS all health services were free for all residents of the United Kingdom. Since 1948 both the original Act and the administrative structure have been modified several times. By amendments of the Act in 1949 and 1951 a fee of one shilling (14 cents) was placed on prescriptions and small charges were made for dental plates and spectacles except for children, expectant mothers, and persons who could not afford to pay. Since that time the prescription fee has been doubled and the charge for dentures and spectacles has been increased.

Aneurin Bevan, the first Minister of Health under the NHS, resigned in protest against the establishment of these fees in 1951. In 1957 the Minister of Health was given power to require payment for services to persons who come to England specifically for treatment. Medical and hospital care is still given to any visitor who becomes ill or suffers injury while in Britain. Specific arrangements have been made between Britain and Denmark, New Zealand, Norway, Sweden, and Yugoslavia under which nationals of these countries may receive treatment under the NHS and British nationals may receive health benefits under the legislation of those countries.

Nearly the entire population of Britain is using the NHS. The cost of the service totals 933 million pounds ($2,613 million) a year (1960-61). This represents approximately 18 pounds or $50 per capita a year. About 70 per cent of the cost is met from the national treasury, 8 per cent from local taxes, 12½ per cent is from payroll deductions in connection with national insurance, about 5½ per cent from payments in connection with superannuation schemes and 4½ per cent is borne by the charges to patients mentioned above.[86]

The organization of the NHS is rather complex and all-inclusive. It is, however, highly decentralized. One hundred and thirty-eight local executive councils in England and Wales are responsible for the administration and general management of the family practitioner services, and fifteen regional hospital boards are in general charge of the hospital and specialist services. The local Executive Councils have twenty-five members, twelve of whom are appointed by the local doctors; eight are appointed by the local health authority and five by the Minister of Health. These councils are in general concerned with the rules and regulations of the NHS. They work closely with the local Medical Practitioner Committees which are more concerned with matters of professional ethics.[87]

The regional Hospital Boards have a membership of between twenty-two and thirty-two persons. Each Board is located near and associated with a university school of medicine. The members are appointed by the Minister after consultation with universities, local health authorities, professional medical associations, certain voluntary health associations, employers, and trade unions.

The local health authorities which have been mentioned above are essentially the county and city health departments which had been functioning for many years before the NHS. They provide such services as: maternity and child welfare, social work and visiting nurses, vaccination, home nursing, domestic help, ambulances, and preventive measures. They are also in charge of local health centers.

The family doctor service, that is, general practice, is the backbone of the NHS. In 1961 there were 20,188 "principals" (fully qualified experienced doctors) and 1,169 "assistants" (completing training) in the family doctor service.[88] Patients may choose the doctor they wish and may change doctors if they so desire. The patient may also go to any doctor in the service for assistance in case he is away from home. The doctor has a similar freedom to accept or refuse patients as he wishes. He cannot be compelled to treat a person against his will, although he has a professional obligation to provide treatment where necessary. The doctor is free to attend to private paying patients if he cares to do so in addition to his regular NHS patients.[89] There are no regulations or controls influencing the doctor's treatment of patients or in prescribing. There is provision for investigating "improper or excessive" prescribing. These judgments are made by the doctors' professional colleagues.

The general practitioner is free to consult with specialists when he thinks it necessary and of course may refer a patient to the hospital without any reference to outside authority. Doctors who were practicing before the NHS usually continued to practice in the same community. Now, "any doctor wishing to take up NHS practice must first get the consent of the Medical Practices Committee in case there should be a sufficient number of doctors in the area already. It is one of the aims of the National Health Service to improve distribution of doctors so that everyone may have an equal chance of first class medical attention; it is therefore essential to apply some limit to the number of practitioners in any given area. Doctors are not told where they should practice, however, and refusals of permission are not very common."[90] The Medical Practices Committee mentioned in this quotation is a national body appointed by the Minister, after consultation with representative professional organizations. It consists of a chairman and eight other members. The Chairman and six members must be medical practitioners, and five of the six must actually be in practice.

Each doctor has or acquires a list of patients. Practices are built up and maintained in the same ways that are common in private practice. Many new doctors take over existing practices of retired or deceased doctors. Others enter existing partnerships. Practices can not be bought. The average number of patients on doctors' lists is now approximately 2,300.[91] A doctor's remuneration is based upon how many patients he has on his roll—not on how many patients he sees. In 1957, the "capitation payment" was 17 shillings a year with an additional 10 shillings for every patient within the range of 501 to 1,500 on the doctor's list, plus special allowances. It was in 1957 that a dispute arose between the doctors and the government about levels of payment. Since remuneration has been a continuing problem, it may be well to review briefly the background of the dispute.[92]

In 1946, Aneurin Bevan, the Minister of Health, in preparation for inaugurating the National Health Service, appointed a committee, the function of which was to make recommendations on remuneration of general practitioners, consultants, and specialists. This committee was known as the Spens Committee. It made two reports, one in 1946 and one in 1948. In these reports, the committee made recommendations as to the proper levels of pay for the two branches of the profession and was concerned also with maintaining levels of remuneration in the future, which were to be set after taking into consideration the value of money, that is, real purchasing power at the time. These recommendations were accepted by the doctors and by the existing Labour government as the basis upon which the profession entered the NHS. The legal status of the Spens report, however, remained in question.

In March, 1952, after adjudication by Mr. Justice Danckwerts, which gave effect to the Spens Committee's recommendations for general practitioners (taking into account the change in value of money from 1939), a "betterment award" of 100 per cent was made, above the 1939 levels. The Minister of Health accepted the award as just, but pointed out that there was no justification for any assumption that such a raise represented an appropriate standard of remuneration for all professionals in the country. By 1954, all three branches of the profession—general practitioners, consultants and specialists, and hospital staff —had received comparable salary increases.

In June, 1956, the profession submitted notice of intention to request increases in salary according to the Spens Committee agreement. The Minister of Health and the government (now Conservative) took the view that the remuneration of the medical profession, like that of others, must be determined from time to time in the light of all relevant circumstances, and that in the present circumstances they would not feel justified in giving consideration to any increase in medical remuneration. The doctors considered that the Spens Committee report, which had been accepted by the government, represented a contractual obligation to the profession. The government denied this, and charges were made in Parliament that the medical profession was trying to isolate itself from the effects of inflation which were felt by other working groups.

Mr. D. Vosper was appointed Minister of Health in 1957. The doctors pressed the new Minister for a 24 per cent raise, which had been arrived at in keeping with the Spens report.

The Minister announced that a Royal Commission would be set up to review medical and dental remuneration. The doctors did not consider a Royal Commission to be the proper agency to consider their claims and suggested that some form of arbitration be used to settle the dispute. In February of that year the General Medical Services Committee of the BMA recommended the resignation of general practitioners from the National Health Service if the government did not agree to "immediate and satisfactory settlement of claim or, alternatively, arbitration." This recommendation was later endorsed by the British Medical Association Council and, in addition, they resolved not to cooperate with the Royal Commission.

In April, 1957, Mr. Macmillan announced that the government had decided to grant an increase of 5 per cent to all doctors and dentists. The doctors called this an arbitrary decision without previous consultation with representatives of the profession which, in accordance with the Spens report, it was obliged to do. Also, they maintained that the cost of living had gone up by 24 per cent since the previous adjustment. They recommended that the 5 per cent increase be placed in a "suspense account" and reiterated their desire for arbitration. However, after the Royal Commission had issued a statement on how it intended to proceed, the doctors changed their minds and decided that they would give evidence before the Royal Commission. The profession was not, of course, obliged to accept its decision. Also at this point the British Medical Association set up a committee to conduct an over-all study of the NHS with the aim of "eradicating those faults of the present system which cause dissatisfaction to the public . . .," not to do away with it.

In June, 1957, at a special representative meeting of the BMA, the position of cooperating with the Royal Commission was confirmed, and withdrawal from the NHS was deferred.

July 16 of the same year, at the BMA's annual representative meeting, a "draft plan" was drawn up which was to be submitted later to the BMA Study Committee mentioned above. The draft proposed certain changes in method of payment, instituting charges for some medicines and modifications in administration of the program. In presenting the draft to the meeting, Dr. H. H. D. Sutherland stressed its tentative nature and that the public interest was uppermost. He said that no significant changes in the NHS were expected in the next five to ten years.

The problem was finally settled in 1960. Doctors are now paid according to the recommendations of the Royal Commission which was set up in 1957. The Commission reported in February, 1960, and in April, 1960, H.M. Government declared themselves willing to accept the recommendations as a whole, provided that the doctors and dentists, respectively, were ready to accept them on the same basis. Officers of the Ministry of Health then met with representatives of the professions in order that a clear and comprehensive picture of the possible effects of the proposals might be put before their members. The medical profession accepted the proposals at a special meeting of the Representative Body of the British Medical Association in September, 1960.

The recommendations of the Royal Commission on the payment of doctors providing general medical services under the NHS were made after comparing the earnings of doctors and dentists with those of other professions. The average net income from all official sources, as recommended by the Commission, is 2,425 pounds for general practitioners under the age of seventy.

General practitioners are paid from a Central Pool the size of which is determined by multiplying the average net remuneration (2,425 pounds) by the number of doctors under seventy who provide unrestricted general medical services; some addition is made in respect of practice expenses, while deduction is also made to take account of earnings from hospitals, local authorities and other official sources outside the NHS.

Actual payment is made by the local Executive Council in whose area the doctor works. The Executive Council receives its share of the Central Pool after amounts have been set aside for the Rural Practices Fund and for Initial Practice Allowances, etc.

The recommendations of the Royal Commission, which became effective on January 1, 1960, did not include a detailed scheme for the distribution of the Central Pool. The details which follow were worked out by representatives of the Health

Departments and the medical profession and went into effect in 1961. The general practitioner's chief remuneration still comes from *capitation fees* at a standard rate which was raised from 17 shillings to 19 shillings and 6 pence per annum for every patient on his list. The maximum number of patients which a general practitioner may accept under the NHS remained 3,500 for a single-handed practitioner; 4,500 for a member of a partnership; and an additional 2,000 if a permanent assistant is employed. An additional payment of 14 shillings is made for each person within the range of 401 to 1,600 (501 to 1,700 in the case of a partnership) on the list. Doctors may receive additional payments for services as detailed in the agreement.[93]

The general practitioner practicing in a partnership, which is the most common form of practice, having the average number of patients, would thus receive approximately 3,140 pounds, or $8,792. This calculation does not include income from private patients. Although most general practitioners have a few such patients, the fees do not amount to very much. Doctors having a full list, in partnership arrangement, which is not uncommon, would receive approximately $15,000 a year.

Discussion

The NHS has been subject to almost continual criticism, both from the British and from outside the country, from the time of its inception to the present. The criticism may be divided into three kinds according to the major concern evidenced: ideological, professional, and organizational.

The ideological criticism is of course part of the larger contemporary problem of defining the proper service functions of the state. It is sometimes made to appear to be a part of the even larger struggle between totalitarianism and democracy. This context is totally inappropriate. The association of "socialized medicine" with socialism and socialism with communism and totalitarianism is clearly a naïve propaganda technique which is employed for political purposes. It would seem unnecessary to draw attention to the fact that comprehensive social welfare functions including health care have been assumed by democratic countries such as England, Sweden, Norway,

Denmark, New Zealand, Australia, Canada, Israel, and West Germany as well as the Soviet Union, Yugoslavia, and Spain.

Nevertheless, there remains in the minds of many people the question whether or not health services should be a public responsibility and thus included among the legitimate functions of the state. Some maintain that if the indigent are cared for, medical services for the rest of the population should be on a competitive, ability-to-pay basis. Others are committed to the proposition that everyone regardless of ability to pay has a right to services essential to the maintenance of health. In the United States we accept the principle of free public education, but we have not extended this principle to health. Most civilized countries in the world, whether or not they have developed adequate public programs of medical care, have accepted the principle of state responsibility for health care.

In England the Beveridge Report was accepted by the Coalition Government of Winston Churchill, and, although the NHS was inaugurated under a Labour government, the Conservatives and Liberals still properly take much credit for it. The fact that the service has never been a political issue since 1948 is evidence of the wide acceptance of the principle of public medical care.

Our research,[94] as well as English studies, have indicated that there are very few people in England, including doctors, who do not accept the principle of public responsibility. Although the analysis of our 1962 study is not complete, it is clear that not more than 2 or 3 per cent of the doctors interviewed rejected the principle of "socialized medicine." Both the BMA and the Medical Practitioners Union fully accept the principle. The Ross Survey of 1952 in England found only 5 per cent of the population opposed to the NHS. Social Survey in 1956 found 90 per cent favorable, 7 per cent undecided and 3 per cent against.[95]

The criticism which is centered on technical and professional problems of medical care is concerned largely with the relationship of the medical profession to the state and the dangers of political influence in medical practice. This problem has been discussed at some length in a preceding paper.[96] It may suffice to say at this point that the nationalization of a profession is a matter of utmost seriousness and every safeguard must be employed to avoid encroachment of political decisions upon professional areas of practice.

On the whole, the NHS has been quite successful in avoiding political interference in medical practice. The doctor is completely free to diagnose, prescribe, and treat according to his own judgment. In fact our recent study indicates that the doctors now have a wider freedom in prescribing than they had in private practice. This is, of course, because they now prescribe without regard to cost to the patient. They also have easier access to specialists and consultants than they previously enjoyed. Hospitalization is more easily utilized than it was under private medicine. And, although hospital space is in short supply, and there are waiting lists for admittance, we did not interview a single doctor who, after he had made the medical decision that hospitalization was necessary, had experienced any difficulty in gaining admittance for his patient.

There is a pressing need for more hospital beds. But the situation is much improved over what it was in 1948 and is much better than it would have been if the hospitals had not been nationalized. In 1948 there were 2,800 out-of-date hospitals in England. They were dependent upon private and municipal funds for support. It is generally conceded that private funds could not have been found to enlarge and modernize these hospitals. This work has been carried on with public funds, and present plans call for ninety new and 134 remodeled hospitals by 1970.[97]

In our recent study[98] many doctors expressed their gratitude for public support of hospitals, pointing out that the situation would have been impossible without it.

There is much evidence that professionalism in medicine, with all that term implies, is now at a higher level in England than ever before. The elimination of all pecuniary considerations is of course a great boon to professionalism, and the increased freedom to prescribe and treat which this permits has given rise to a high level of medical practice.

Most of the continuing criticism of the NHS by doctors and

others is concerned with problems of organization and administration. We found that these criticisms are almost always in
vague general terms. For example a doctor might say: "There
should be some means of cutting down our lists and at the
same time retaining our present income," or "Under the present
organization a few patients tend to abuse the service. There
should be some way to prevent these people from using our
time unnecessarily."[99]

In this connection it is interesting to observe that the
doctor's definition of what constitutes an abuse has changed.
In private practice, a mother's call for the doctor to see her
child suffering from a slight cough or sore throat was thought
to be the act of an intelligent, loving young woman. Now the
same call may be defined as an abuse. Doctors in England, as
everywhere, work long hours. Many are certainly "overworked."
Now that their remuneration is based upon the number of
. patients on their lists rather than upon the number of patients
they see, there is a tendency to resent the calls for minor
ailments. When questioned, however, they do freely concede
the substantial advantage enjoyed under the present system in
seeing cases early in their development. A common complaint
of doctors, both here and abroad, has been that people do not
see a doctor early enough. The NHS has no doubt made a great
contribution to preventive medicine by facilitating early diagnosis and treatment.

Other dissatisfactions with the present organization of the
NHS concern financial remuneration. Some are critical of the
present arrangements which were accepted by both the profession and the government in 1960. Many doctors in the London
area feel that there should be some "loading system" to compensate for the higher cost of living in that area. Although
this seems reasonable, any attempt to relate payment to local
costs of living would become hopelessly complicated administra-
tively. Additional payments are now given to doctors practicing
in designated less desirable places, and mileage allowance is
made to rural doctors. There is a rather widespread feeling
among general practitioners that their income is not as high as
it should be, or that they have to have more patients on their

lists than they would like in order to receive "adequate" income.[100]

It is our impression that the dissatisfaction, where it exists, arises from comparison with the incomes of executives in business and industry and the differential tax situation. The doctors' income compares favorably with those of other professions and with higher positions in the civil service.

The NHS has sometimes been attacked on the grounds that it places too heavy a tax burden on the public. In the early 1950's, when it became clear that the service would cost more than had been anticipated, a large portion of public opinion expressed fears of excessive cost. The British Medical Journal said editorially, "The National Health Service is heading for the bankruptcy court . . . because of the Utopian finances of the Welfare State."[101] The Government reacted to this public concern about the cost by setting up a committee of inquiry in 1953 to review the whole matter of financing the service. At the request of the committee a detailed study was made by the National Institute of Economic and Social Research, a well-known private organization. Most of the responsibility for the study was assumed by B. Abel-Smith and R. M. Titmuss. Their findings were accepted by the committee and included in the committee report,[102] known as the Guillebaud Report. They found that the "rising cost of the service in real terms during the years 1948-54 had been kept within narrow bounds." Charges of widespread extravagance were not borne out by the evidence.[103] The cost per capita remained almost the same from 1949 to 1954 and the per cent of gross national product spent on all public health care actually decreased: 1949-50, 3.75; 1950-51, 3.71; 1951-52, 3.48; 1952-53, 3.34; 1953-54, 3.24; 1954-55, 3.14; 1955-56, 3.23.[104]

Prof. Lindsey says in a recent book, "The amazing thing is that the cost of medical care in England under the National Health Service at no time has been more than four per cent of the national income. Many other nations spend a larger proportion. Among them is the United States, which in 1959 expended a total of 4.5 per cent of her national income on medical care."[105]

The cost is apparently not "out of line" and criticism on this basis seems unjustified and shortsighted in consideration of the greatly expanded services and the huge savings to the nation which accrue through improved health of the population—not to mention the lessening of human suffering.[106]

Internally, the NHS and the principles upon which it is based are nearly universally accepted. The criticism is almost entirely confined to relatively minor administrative problems. It should be kept in mind that such criticism of a public institution in a democratic society is not only well within the normal expectations, but is a necessary function in determining changes which are essential to ensure the continued success of the institution in meeting the needs for which it was originally established.

The external criticism, that is, from other countries, particularly the United States, has been largely uninformed and frequently irresponsible. The American Medical Association, in its zeal to defeat any move toward expanded public health care in the United States, is responsible for many of the erroneous ideas which are held in this country about the British NHS. The British view (or at least the view of the BMA) of the activities of the AMA were expressed in a recent editorial in the *British Medical Journal* which began: "The American Medical Association is not without critics in its own country, and we may be confident that a great many doctors in the USA deplore, as we do, the vulgarity and cheapness of its past and present attacks on the National Health Service [in their effort to] defeat what our American colleagues call 'socialized medicine.'" The editorial continued by citing instances of "nonsense about the NHS" which has appeared in AMA publications and mentions the *Times* (London) editorial which said: "If the AMA have any regard for the truth, they should put the record straight; the American people should know that far from being a failure the British service can be counted a qualified success."[107]

Various populations define health in different ways. Meanings of illness and expectations of health are related to basic cultural themes in a society and to the existing social structure. Consciousness of health depends in part upon the existence and the availability of health services. In England a portion of the population—largely the working class—had come to "accept" illness, dental defects, and opthalmic deficiencies as "their lot." Now that health services are more accessible, a heightened awareness of illness and the value of health has occurred.

The situation is analagous to education. As long as a grammar school education was outside the realm of possibility for most working class children, a personal awareness of the value of such an education was likely to be lacking. Postwar changes in secondary education, which are to be discussed in the following section, have broadened educational expectations as the NHS has expanded expectations in regard to health.

Education: English Secondary Education and the Social Class Structure[*]

a) Theoretical Frame of Reference and Historical Perspective

Education in the broadest sense may be thought of as the institutionalized as well as the informal universal process of passing on the culture of a society and socializing its individuals. The school, in addition to these conserving functions, may also be an innovating force in society. It may cause or impede social change. It may buttress existing economic and political structures or it may subtly or more directly engender revolution. In relation to a system of social stratification, the school may either provide a means for mobility or it may perpetuate the established status arrangements—or both. As Floud and Halsey have pointed out, education and the school may produce unintended as well as intended, and dysfunctional as well as functional consequences; it may function in some respects as a relatively independent variable.[108]

In sociological terms, education may be thought of as having two characteristic functions in relation to existing systems of social

---

[*] Presented at a Conference on English Education, U.S. Office of Education, Department of Health, Education and Welfare, Washington, D.C., 1960, and published in *Education in England, Studies in Comparative Education*, Dept. of H. E. and W., Office of Education, Washington, 1961.

stratification: differentiation and selection.[109] In caste and estate societies the major function of education is to maintain the existing system of social differentiation and to perpetuate differential social evaluation of differentiated statuses. The young are prepared to assume their proper places and roles according to the dictates of society. Class societies by definition being to some degree open societies, provide a setting in which the major function of the school is or can be in social selection. Modern industrial societies profess, in some version and in varying degree, an ideology of egalitarianism and equality of opportunity. In such societies intergenerational movement up or down in the class structure is considered to be right and proper. Modern industrial societies are furthermore confronted with problems of great complexity, sometimes accompanied by a sense of urgency, in the selection, education, and employment of persons in ways thought to be essential to the on-going of a society characterized by a high degree of division of labor and technological specialization.

Two ideal types of schools, then, may be constructed: (1) the estate-system school whose major function is in maintaining and perpetuating the existing system of differential statuses, and (2) the class-system school whose primary purposes are associated with selection, mobility, and social change. It may be useful to keep these constructed types in mind in this discussion of contemporary English secondary schools.

Although European nations, including England, have in the past seen the school as an adaptive agency traditionally serving a differentiating function, they are now becoming more and more aware of education in its selective and innovating roles. Everywhere there is a growing concern about "the waste of human talent." England is no exception to this awareness.

In order to comment upon contemporary English education in relation to the existing class structure it is necessary first to briefly (and I fear somewhat superficially) review in abbreviated historical perspective the rise of social classes in Britain. The term class will be used here to refer to segments of the population which are differentiated not only by economic criteria, but also by style of life. Certain amounts of prestige and power are correlates of class, but in this paper these aspects of class must remain implicit.[110] Classes are of course open and in class societies some amount of mobility between the classes is within the normal expectations of the culture.

Without attempting an historical analysis, historical perspective may be gained by drawing attention to the transition from an estate society to a class society which accompanied the commercial and industrial revolutions.[111] In broad outline, a large portion of the medieval estate of farm labor became an urban proletariat over a period of time, in response to changes in land usage as well as to the factory system. They composed a free working class. These workers then found themselves a part of an industrial society characterized by a growing rationality, secularization and bureaucratization which was slowly replacing the traditional "sacred society" of the Middle Ages. The new class arrangements and the differential distribution of objective privilege which they represented were rationalized by nineteenth-century political and economic doctrines and ideologies. These arrangements were further justified by the Protestant Ethic and social Darwinism.

Social inequality in the early industrial period became almost a religion. R. H. Tawney, in his notable book *Equality*,[112] titles the first chapter "The Religion of Inequality," and credits Matthew Arnold with using the phrase at about the turn of the century. However, others, not so perceptive, or of a different turn of mind, were defending the existing class arrangements as functional and, indeed, necessary for the integration and on-going of the society. Bagehot argued that the secret of English political institutions was in the fact that they had been created by a "differential people."[113] The Bishop of London reported in 1803, "Men of considerable ability say that it is safest for both the government and the religion of the country to let the lower classes remain in that state of ignorance in which nature has originally placed them."[114] Thring, founder of the Headmasters' Conference, assuaged the apprehension of the upper classes at the extension of education by arguing that the "law of labour" compels the majority of children to work for wages at the age of ten, and that "it is not possible that a class which is compelled to leave off training at ten years of age can oust, by superior intelligence, a class which is able to spend four more years in acquiring skill."[115]

The exploitation of the working class in the early period of industrial capitalism needs no documentation. The people were insecure, unhealthy, ill-housed, and uneducated.

The transition from an estate society to a class society brought with it a new set of human relationships. The rising industrial class was in some respects not much more secure than were the workers. It is true that they came to dominate the economic and political process, but their new power was not accompanied by comparable gains in prestige which remained largely with the landed aristocracy. This uncertain social position gave rise to middle-class humanitarianism. The ignoble business classes became conspicuous subscribers to charity work which sometimes approached the *noblesse oblige* of the aristocracy. Philanthropies, child-saving organizations, settlement houses, and organized charities were pursued in large part as a means of acquiring prestige and increased social honor in the society. Engels, in *The Condition of the Working Class in England in 1844*, refers to these activities as "parasitic philanthropy."[116] They had, however, wider implications. It was through such charitable activities that eighteenth-century "dame schools" and "parish schools" came to be augmented by the charity schools, "ragged schools," and Sunday schools which formed the spearhead against the illiteracy of the working class. In 1833 Parliament began to make annual grants to the voluntary societies which were providing schools and the Elementary Education Act of 1870 accepted the principle of compulsory education. By the end of the nineteenth century elementary education had become virtually compulsory and available to all, free of charge. Public provision of secondary education was started in England under the Act of 1902. The next major reorganization was the Education Act of 1944.[117]

b) The 1944 Education Act and its Social-Class Implications

The second part of this study is devoted to a discussion of this Act and its social class implications. (The third part of the study will be concerned with the present functioning of the private grammar schools.)

The 1944 Education Act grew out of a long-existing concern about the condition of the working class which sometimes paralleled *noblesse oblige* and middle-class humanitarianism, but which was motivated by a very different spirit and pursued in a strikingly different fashion. A small group of intellectuals, mostly of middle-class background, initiated and carried on a remarkable series of social surveys in England during the latter part of the nineteenth and the early twentieth century. The social survey has been defined in England in a peculiarly limited way. Both A. F. Wells[118] and D. Caradog Jones[119] define the social survey as a fact-finding study, *dealing chiefly with the conditions of the working class.* From the time of the original study by Charles Booth, *Life and Labour of the People of London,* 1889 and 1902, through the work of Rowntree, the Webbs and Bowley to the *New Survey of London Life and Labour,* 1930-35, and the Beveridge Report, a mass of data revealed that great inequalities existed between the classes. Although the social surveys were not concerned with education per se, it soon became apparent that in large part the differential social and economic conditions could be laid to the nature of the educational system. The English system of schools (if, indeed they could be called a system) had been functioning for many generations largely as a differentiating agency which perpetuated the traditional class structure of the early industrial period. The Fabian Society not only came to this conclusion but further pointed out that this situation was clearly incompatible with the requirements of a modern democratic industrial society. More recent and more sophisticated studies have, in a general way, come to the same conclusions. D. V. Glass has brought together some of this work in *Social Mobility in Britain.*[120] English scholars have developed measuring devices such as the concepts of "perfect mobility,"[121] "ability/opportunity ratios"[122] and "class chances."[123] Class chances of mobility are determined by relating the social composition of educational institutions and occupational groups to that of the population from which they are recruited. This method has revealed marked discrepancies between the classes in educational opportunities.[124]

The Labour Party, for which the Fabians furnished much of the ideology in its earlier years, has been much concerned with these educational problems. However, they were not alone as was shown by the fact that the 1944 Education Act was passed by the coalition government under Winston Churchill.

One other point, which cannot be elaborated here: the 1944 Education Act should be seen as an integral part of the legislation which brought the welfare state into being.[125] D. V. Glass has pointed out, "What we wish to do in the field of education should not, and cannot, be kept apart from our broader social objectives —from our ideas of the kind of society we wish to see develop."[126] Education is of necessity a basic part of the program to provide employment, health, and security for the entire population through social and economic planning.

The 1944 Education Act replaced the former dual division of public education—elementary and higher education—with a three-stage system—primary, secondary, and "further education." Under the new arrangements the educational process was, for the first time, to be considered a continuous one through which all children and young people will pass.* In the Act, emphasis is placed upon providing free public secondary education for all children between the ages of eleven and fifteen. Three types of secondary schools were to be established—Grammar, Modern and Technical. The idea of separation of children in the secondary schools goes back to the Hadow Report of 1926. This report proposed a complete break for all children at the age of eleven and their assignment to separate schools. In 1938 the Spens Report furthered the concept of separation by proposing the technical high school as an alternative type of secondary school which would admit children at the age of eleven.

The White Paper, *Educational Reconstruction*,[127] is evidence

---

* "It was not till 1944 that, with the statutory recognition of primary education as no longer the education of a particular class of children, but merely one stage in the education of all children, these senile abortions, at once inhuman and grotesque, of English educational snobbery ceased, at last, at least in theory, to cumber the ground." R. H. Tawney, *Equality*, George Allen and Unwin, London, 4th edition, 1952, p. 247.

that the Act was conceived of as a means of widening educational opportunity—of providing every child the kind of education best suited to his needs and capacities. In our frame of reference the new secondary schools and the system of allocation were thought of, at the time of their inception, as representing a significant movement away from the conception of education as having primarily a differentiating function toward increasing emphasis upon the selective function. The school was no longer to be a dependent and adaptive variable in society.

R. A. Butler is quoted as saying, in reference to the 1944 Education Bill before it became law, that education cannot by itself create the social structure of a country. Nevertheless, he continued, "It can very considerably influence it and I believe the fact that we have got a priority for this great Bill will very much influence the world in which we hope to live in the future."[128]

The Central Advisory Council for Education, 1959, said, "Today it seems to us that education is generally thought to be a 'nation building' investment. . . ."[129] Also, such statements as the following were being made, "The courage and imagination with which the development plan is drawn, the energy and judgment with which it is carried into effect, will not only determine the future of our educational system, but may largely shape the future course of the nation's forward march."[130] For the first time the Minister of Education was given "effective power to secure development of the national policy in education."[131] The Labour Party and socialists generally were, at first, fairly well satisfied with the Act.

It should be noted that eighteen years had passed since the Hadow Report, and that the report made in 1926 was based upon a psychology of previous decades. The psychology of the early 1900's cannot be discussed here, but, among other things, and particularly after 1918, it was psychology which gave much more credence to the results of intelligence testing than has been the case in later years. These tests were thought by many to be culture-free, almost invariable measures of innate capacity. The social influences on the distribution of measured intelligence were either not known or were not taken into account. There were, on the other hand, what might be referred to as cultural compulsions, deep-seated in English society, which tended to promulgate a segregated, differentiating system of schools.

Having set up a tripartite system of secondary schools—it was not truly a tripartite system, because the technical schools were not comparable to the grammar and modern schools—the educational authorities were faced with the problem of selection of pupils. A battery of tests was devised in which an intelligence test plays an important part. The form varies somewhat but usually a test of achievement, in the form of two papers, one in English composition and one in arithmetic, is included. This examination is administered to all children in the last year of primary school, which means at the age of eleven-plus. The child's score on this examination largely determines which type of secondary school he will attend. The students acquiring the highest scores attend grammar schools. However, they may choose to attend a technical school. The remainder, constituting roughly 60 to 70 per cent of the total age group, attend secondary modern schools.

The traditional prestige of the grammar schools must be kept in mind. Many of the new state-supported grammar schools were previously church-related private schools and all of them are patterned upon the old high-status, independent private schools. It is generally considered that if a boy or girl does not obtain a score which will permit him to attend a grammar school he has *failed* the examination. Failure to attend a grammar school effectively eliminates the possibility of the student entering the professions, higher grades of the civil service, and many positions in business and industry. J. D. Scott describes the situation as follows:

> The grammar schools are [with the private schools] universally recognized to be producing the future leadership. Most of the well-paid, responsible, interesting jobs will go to grammar school boys and girls. These schools have accordingly a high prestige and the examination which is held at the age of eleven to twelve to decide what kind of secondary school a child shall go to is, for all ambitious parents, simply a competition for entry into a grammar school. For many middle-class parents, who would be only too happy to pay grammar school fees, but who cannot

afford the fees charged by the public [private] schools, this examination is a nightmare, since failure—that is failure to get into a grammar school—is taken to mean a kind of proletarianisation of the children.[132]

This quotation represents, in common terms, a very widespread evaluation of the new system and the selection procedures. It should also be pointed out that many of the middle-class parents whose children fail to be selected for a grammar school—if they can possibly afford it—send them to fee-charging private grammar schools. These "failures" may not be able to get into the old high-status private schools but they are being accepted in private schools of the grammar school type. In fact, new private schools are being established largely for the purpose of receiving them.

This situation, along with the social class bias of the examination, results in some degree of segregation of secondary students by social class. The report of the Central Advisory Council for Education, 1959, states that "The grammar school as it is in the first five years of the course is socially a pretty fair cross-section of the population."[133] The term "pretty fair" is a loose one and probably is used here to indicate that most grammar school children are of working-class origin. This is apparently true, but the work of Halsey and Floud, referred to above, has shown that the working class is still under-represented in relation to the size of the working class in England—which is variously determined to be from 70 to 75 per cent of the population. In terms of "class chances" the working class suffers from differential opportunity. The fact that there are large grammar schools in urban working-class residential districts which are composed almost exclusively of working-class children makes the overall picture appear to be somewhat more heterogeneous than many of the grammar schools in reality are. The secondary modern school, on the other hand, has a disproportionately high representation from the working class.

Criticism of the 1944 Act became very widespread in a relatively short time. In 1953 the Labour Party pledged itself to do away with the whole system and establish comprehensive schools. "Labour will abolish the practice of selection at eleven-plus for different types of schools because it is convinced that all children would benefit if, during the whole of the period of their secondary education, they shared the facilities, both social and educational, of one comprehensive school."[134]

Although there are, under the 1944 Act, many more working-class children in grammar schools in England than ever before, nevertheless it appears to many that the new system is largely perpetuating the class structure. The system of schools which had been motivated by a radical desire to broaden opportunities, reduce class differences,* and bring about a closer relationship between ability, function, and status in society, was now thought by many not only to have failed but to have resulted in heightening social differences. Edward Blishen, speaking before the Council for Children's Welfare in London recently said, "When we divide children at eleven-plus, we divide men from men. . . . It is all wrong to have children between the ages of eleven and fifteen thinking of themselves as the head or the tail."[135]

D. V. Glass observed in 1953:

> . . . The Act . . . will by no means minimize the disadvantages of the new unstable relationships between successive generations. On the contrary, the more efficient the selection procedure, the more evident those disadvantages are likely to become. Outside of the public [private] schools, it will be the grammar schools which will furnish the new *elite*, an elite apparently much less assailable because it is selected for measured intelligence. The selection process will tend to reinforce the prestige of occupations already high in social status and to divide the population into streams which many may come to regard— indeed may already regard—as distinct as sheep and goats. Not to have been to a grammar school will be a more serious disqualification than in the past, when social inequality in the education system was known to exist. And the feeling of resentment may be more rather than less acute just because the individual concerned realizes that there is some validity in the

---

* The White Paper, *Educational Reconstruction,* had not only pointed out the need for equality of educational opportunity and for a diversity to suit various abilities, it also emphasized that "such diversity must not impair the social unity within the educational system which will open the way to a more closely knit society . . ." p. 3.

selection process which has kept him out of a grammar school. In this respect, apparent justice may be more difficult to bear than injustice.[136]

As mentioned earlier in this paper, schools may have unintentional as well as intended, and dysfunctional as well as functional, consequences. The prevailing criticisms of the state-supported secondary schools and the selection system may be briefly summarized.

1. It is widely thought that the age of eleven is too young for a child to be subjected to an examination the results of which will greatly influence the rest of his life.

2. The selection procedure engenders a high degree of emotional tension and anxiety in both the child and his family. Rewards are promised for success, and threats are made against failure. Failure, one must keep in mind, is defined by the public as not being selected for a grammar school. This anxiety is not limited to the middle-class parents and children. Now that the possibility exists, a large proportion of the working class have grammar school aspirations for their children.[137]

3. The validity of the examination is being questioned. The technical aspects of the tests are not understood by lay people and they do not trust them. Also, the belief is widespread that children can be coached for the examination, and that some receive better coaching than others. It is apparently true that much of the last term of the primary school is given over to "preparing" the pupils for the selection examination. The tests are open to other criticisms. I.Q. scores, as was indicated above, are thought to be class-biased, thereby placing the working-class child at a disadvantage. British studies have shown a difference of about twenty points between mean scores of the highest and lowest occupational groups. However, the Himmelweit-Whitfield study indicated that differences within occupational groups were greater than between them, except for the highest and lowest status occupations. Halsey, in a study of the relationship between genetics, social structure and intelligence, concludes that:

> [What] we know of the genetics of native intelligence and the history of social mobility in Britain leads us to doubt the hypothesis of innate class differences in main intelligence. . . .

From this and from consideration of the small reduction in the variance of measured intelligence which results from classifying children according to paternal occupation it seems reasonable to conclude that the observed differences between social classes in measured intelligence are more likely to be explained by environmental rather than genetic factors.[138]

Studies of the social influences on the distribution of measured intelligence carried on by Floud and Halsey conclude in the light of present knowledge of these factors ". . . that it would be unethical, as well as uneconomic and impolitic to gear educational selection too closely to test results."[139]

4. The system results in some degree of segregation by social class, the secondary modern schools being very largely working-class and the grammar schools having an over-representation from the middle class. This results not only from the selection system but from the existence of the private grammar school as an alternative to the secondary modern for middle-class children.[140] This is the essence of the criticism by the Labour Party.

5. A further criticism of the selection program is that, even if the examination were selective on the basis of ability, other factors, such as the number of places available in local grammar schools in relation to the size of the age group, may determine the cutting point. In one local district, all children making an I.Q. score above 110 may be admitted to the grammar school, whereas in a locality having more limited facilities, an I.Q. of 115 or 120 may be required. Some research has indicated that these two factors, number of places available and size of the working-class population, are more important than the examination score in selection for grammar schools.[141]

The proportion of grammar school places to the total population varies so greatly from one part of England to another, and bears so varying a relation both to the social background and the distribution of ability in particular communities, that about the only thing one can safely say is that the grammar school will contain the ablest, and the modern school the least able of the boys and girls in its catchment. . . . There is a considerable intermediate group of boys and girls whose abilities would in one place give them a grammar school education and in another a modern school one. There are also everywhere a large number of boys and girls whose performance falls well short of their early promise, and others (probably quite as numerous) whose development exceeds anticipation.[142]

It has also been pointed out that pupils in crowded, poorly equipped rural schools have less chance of obtaining grammar school entrance than do children from city schools. In the County of Buckingham, the disparity is reported to be: 30 to 50 per cent go to grammar schools from the towns and only 2.5 to 10 per cent from the country.[143]

6. Other data which have brought the present system into question have been presented in studies of drop-outs. About 20 per cent of the students selected for grammar schools leave school before they finish, and fewer than half of those who finish the grammar school course pass examinations in five subjects which is the minimum for university matriculation.[144]

These apparent discrepancies between the distribution of intelligence (or ability) by social class and educational opportunity are held by many to represent social class discrimination in contemporary secondary education. If this is a true picture of the situation, it represents a waste of human talent inimical to the best interests of the society.

The original Act of 1944 was written in such a way as to provide for a gradual implementation of the system and for modifications as recommended by the Minister of Education. Study commissions and advisory groups have been almost continuously at work. One of the most recent reports has come from the Central Advisory Council for Education, 1959. This group, after exhaustive study, recommended extension of the age of compulsory school attendance to sixteen and the initiation of a system of "county colleges" in which part-time attendance would be required until the age of eighteen. In looking to the future, this group also says:

> The two-sided system [grammar and modern] is unlikely to survive in the future in the form in which it existed five or six years ago, or to be replaced by a tripartite system of the kind which used to be suggested [grammar, modern and technical]. Once it is agreed, as more and more people are coming to be-

lieve, that it is wrong to label children for all time at 11, the attempt to give mutually exclusive labels to the schools to which they go at that age will have to be abandoned. All over the country changes are being made that profoundly modify the previous pattern of education, and in certain areas, the system is not being modified so much as replaced by a different form of organization. There are many variants . . . we distinguish three . . . because of the contrast of their approach. They are the comprehensive school, the bilateral school and the two-tier organization of secondary education. All aim at reducing the waste of talent . . . all aim at giving each individual pupil a better chance of an education suited to his needs. All have two points of internal organization in common. The first is that all levels of ability are represented in the same school; the second is that all levels of ability are not represented in every class. All . . . provide a common social life; none tries to provide a uniform curriculum.[145]

(These new types of schools will not be discussed as they are considered by other papers in this conference. Their existence, experimentally, and the interest in them does, however, reveal a broadening awareness of the social class biases of the present system.)

c) The Private Grammar Schools and their Social Class Implications

The historic function of the private grammar schools has been one of differentiation. Some of these schools are of medieval origin. Eton was founded in 1440 and Rugby in 1567. Others are even older. Winchester was founded in 1387 and Kings (Canterbury) and St. Peter's (York) are said to go back to Anglo-Saxon times.

Although some were founded as charitable institutions catering, for a time, to poor boys, the major function of most of these schools in the early period was in perpetuating the estate-like society by providing training for the aristocratic life. With the progress of the Industrial Revolution and the transition to a class society, the private grammar schools continued to serve essentially the same function—perpetuation of the stratification system —through giving the proper training for gentlemen. Most of the schools provided for a few free places, but their concern through the years has been to provide an invidious education for the sons of the wealthy whether they be of the landed aristocracy or of the industrial propertied classes.

J. D. Scott says:

> One of the most remarkable things about English education is the persistence, through two world wars, and on into the egalitarian, welfare state world of the fifties, of a separate system of education for the rich. . . . Only in England is education still, quite strictly, a matter of social class, in that it is normal for children of the upper-middle and upper classes to go to a special kind of school in which children of the lower-middle and working classes are rarely met with.[146]

Dr. Glass points out that even though social mobility will be increased by the 1944 Act, it has, by leaving the private system intact, placed a ceiling on upward mobility. Entry to the private schools, he reiterates, is not only by "talent" but also by the wealth of the parents. These schools instill upper class mannerisms and most important of all, a speech accent which carries well-defined social status implications.[147]

The English are acutely aware of speech and dress as status symbols. And, although many people, through personal effort or informal association, have developed bilingual speech to the point where they can use the proper accent at the proper time in the proper places to the right people, nevertheless the "authentic," "natural" speech of the upper classes is most easily acquired through the private schools and upper-class associations. These schools pass on a distinctive way of life which is seldom free of an element of snobbery.

The Labour Party—which it must be kept in mind speaks for nearly half of the population—has repeatedly attacked the private schools as an anachronism in an egalitarian society. Lord Altrincham, prominent Conservative, writing on "A New Toryism," has suggested that, "with their [the old private schools] valuable traditions and large endowments, they should now be at the service of the nation, not simply of a class. . . . Their human content should be revolutionized; instead of the children of well-to-do parents, who may not be capable of profiting (except in a bogus, social sense) from the best secondary education, a growing proportion of scholars should come from the state primary schools. And of course this scheme should be financed by the Exchequer. . . ."[148]

Norwood, in *The English Tradition of Education*, argues that the private schools are successful because they impart a character which is consistent and can be trusted. He also adds: "Other less praiseworthy reasons for success of these schools are that they confer a social badge and give rights of entry to circles which people do as a matter of fact very much desire to enter."[149]

There are 249 independent private secondary schools in England which are officially recognized as efficient.[150] There are a good many others which are not included in this category. Approximately 8 per cent of secondary school children are in private schools. Most of the discussion concerns the thirty or forty of these schools which have the highest social status and are deemed by many to be superior to the state-supported grammar schools.

In the 1930's the enrollment in many of the schools dropped considerably. In 1942 the Fleming Committee was appointed at the request of the private schools to advise the Minister of Education, R. A. Butler, on means "whereby the association between the public [private] schools and the general educational system of the country could be developed and extended."[151] The Committee included among others the Archbishop of Canterbury, the Headmaster of Eton and Professor G. D. H. Cole. It was, no doubt, thought at that time that increasingly few parents would have either the income or the inclination to spend large sums of money on the education of their children. Consequently, the private schools were contemplating some reforms which would preserve their independence but would make them available to a broader section of the community.

The report of this committee in 1944 produced two alternative recommendations. Under the first, both day and boarding schools would receive direct grants from local educational authorities which would enable them to abolish all tuition and boarding fees or, if that was not possible, the fees were to be set on a sliding scale by using a means test. Local educational authorities would reserve places by agreement with the school, but the governors of the school would select the children for the remaining places. All children were to be admitted on the basis of capacity to profit from this type of education. The second scheme applied to boarding schools only. The governors of the school would make available at least 25 per cent of the places a year to pupils whose parents wanted them to go to a private school and who were chosen by an interviewing board as suitable for the particular school. In this case the fee was to be met by a grant from the Ministry of Education. The governors of the various schools would review the scheme every five years in hopes of increasing the percentage of students from state-supported primary schools.

Neither one of these schemes was ever put into effect, or at least was never tried for a very long period of time. One of the difficulties was that the Fleming Report had included all of the private schools in the Headmasters Conference (about 180) in the plan when probably fewer than half of these schools provided an education which was thought to be superior to the state schools. Also, the problem of selection was never satisfactorily solved. However, probably the major reason that changes were not made at that time was the involvement in World War II and the fact that after the war a rather rapid economic recovery solved the problem of enrollment which had been the major concern before the war. Under pressure from the Labour Party and the spread of egalitarianism in postwar Britain, the Conservative party has proposed, in effect, that the private schools be left free to choose whether or not they will remain as they are or admit a more socially heterogeneous student body and accept direct grants from the Ministry of Education or scholarships from local educational authorities.[152] The old high-status private schools are not suffering at the present time for either lack of students or finances. Many of the newer private schools are also flourishing as a result of accepting middle-class children who failed to be selected for the state-supported grammar schools.

The Labour Party has said that "Our aim is to end privilege in education, but because our object is to level up and not to level down, our socialist attack on educational inequality will concentrate, in the first instance, not on abolishing fee-paying schools, but on improving the standards of our free education.[153] It appears that in the second instance the Labour Party might be interested in abolishing the private schools. D. V. Glass has said "So long as the public boarding schools in particular remain outside the State system of secondary education, the 1944 Act cannot fulfill the explicit intention of the White Paper on Educational Reconstruction to provide equality of educational opportunity. And the inequality is likely to cut across the line of social mobility, blocking ascent to, and limiting descent from, the upper reaches of social status."[154]

d) Conclusion: Differentiation and Selection

It is recognized, of course, that most school systems perform both functions—differentiation and selection in relation to societal stratification. Two polar types were constructed and introduced into this discussion for heuristic purposes. These ideal types, in which the two functions are separated, may be reiterated as follows: the estate-system school is perfectly accommodated to the requirements of an essentially static society in performing the functions of social differentiation, and in maintaining and perpetuating the traditional differential social evaluation of differentiated statuses; and, on the other hand, the class-system school is perfectly accommodated to the requirements of an essentially dynamic society in performing the function of social selection compatible with the distribution of native capacity and the concept of perfect mobility. Such a class-system school would encourage social evaluation in relation to social function, and would theoretically eliminate the inheritance of differential statuses. With the attainment of this utopian end it could, of course, no longer be referred to as a class-system school.[155]

In terms of these ideal types, the English secondary schools are performing both the function of differentiation and selection in relation to the stratification system. They are performing a dual role of maintaining existing class arrangements and providing an opportunity for mobility to a minority of the working-class children.

However, the foregoing discussion of the current functioning of the secondary schools under the 1944 Act, along with the role of the private schools, indicates that, on balance, they approach the estate-system school type more closely than they do the class-system type. This is essentially the reason for widespread criticism.

The school is seldom an independent variable. It is so closely interrelated with other institutions and with basic cultural themes in the society that it is much more likely to reflect them than to reshape them. Nevertheless, it is reasonable to assume that rather than any clear-cut cause-and-effect relationship existing it is more apt to be one of reciprocal influence.

Although it is well known that England is, in general terms, a highly industrialized, secularized, and bureaucratized society, it still retains essentially estate-like characteristics. The landed aristocracy, stripped of its power and much of its wealth, has more the appearance of an estate than of a class. Sections of the working class are conscious of their place in society and speak of their "betters." Estate-like symbols of status persist in dress and speech. In England tradition and innovation are conspicuously co-existent. The symbolism of the Royal family, the peerage, socialism, the Trade Union Congress, and the new Toryism all exist side by side. Political-economic planning, regulation and control, individualism and a high regard for personal freedom and civil liberties are all found together. Three-hundred-year-old private charities are being faithfully distributed by the local vicar in the welfare state alongside governmental family allowances and socialized medicine. Church and chapel, Rolls Royce Motors, the Chemical Trust and a million independent shopkeepers carry on as usual. All of this makes it difficult to place contemporary English society precisely on a Weberian charismatic-bureaucratic continuum, or on a Sombartian traditional-rational progression, although, of course, it is far to the rational bureaucratic side.

The direction of change is clear, but at the present time the function of the secondary schools, even the new schools which were created to assist in ushering in the new society, seem to be weighted in the direction of preserving the old.

PART FOUR

COMPARATIVE STUDIES:
Illustrating the use of the concepts class and
nationality, with some implications
for national character

COMPARATIVE PRESTIGE RANKING OF OCCUPATIONS IN AN AMERICAN CITY WITH REFERENCE TO HALL'S AND JONES'S STUDY*

It could be maintained that, theoretically, the prestige of an occupational group is the result of two factors: the functional importance of the occupation and the availability of properly trained personnel. However, every society has derived its own definitions of importance of function in relation to its historical-cultural values and, although the biological distribution of capacity and special talents is similar in various populations, in every society these values and existing social structures place limits upon the opportunity for acquiring special knowledge and experience. If occupational groups are conceived of as functional behavior systems[1] in relation to basic societal values and institutions, it has been assumed that the prestige of occupations will vary from one society to another.

The present study was designed to determine the applicability of certain conclusions of the English study[2] to similar data obtained in the United States. This study is based upon prestige rankings of the same thirty occupations which were ranked in Hall's and Jones's survey. The rankers constituted a sample of 320 adults representative of the city of Spokane, Washington. It parallels, in some respects, the recent studies of Taft in Australia

* From *The British Journal of Sociology*, Vol. V, No. 2, 1954. Published jointly with Bernard Phillips (Pustilnik).

and Congalton in New Zealand, in which these rankings are compared with the "social grading" which was obtained in the
English study.[3]

The data for the study were collected by the Washington
Public Opinion Laboratory as part of a survey conducted in
March, 1952. The random sample of Spokane adult males and
females was stratified by Census Tracts. W.P.O.L. interviewers
presented questionnaires to the respondents with the instructions:
"Please rank the occupations listed below according to your
opinion of their prestige or social standing, by making a check in
the appropriate box—Very High, High, Average, Low, Very Low."

Hall's and Jones's sample consisted of 1,056 adults of which 706
were males. Their major analysis was based on this sample of
male respondents. In making comparisons with the English study,
the writers have used this male sample as the referent. The
English sample was obtained by sending questionnaires to professional and managerial groups, members of adult education
classes and their friends, and to a number of other voluntary
organizations including trade unions. These groups were selected
from various parts of England. The English sample was then
asked to order the occupations as to their social standing, from
one to thirty.[4]

The three conclusions of the English study with which this
study is concerned are: (1) Respondents differ to a greater extent concerning the prestige rankings they accord to occupations
in the central region of the prestige hierarchy than at the top or
bottom of the hierarchy. (2) There is a close correspondence between a hierarchical set of categories of occupations, derived
prior to the research, i.e., the English Standard Classification, and
the empirical judgments of the population sample with respect to
the ordering of occupations on the basis of social standing.
(3) "While there may be minor differences in judgment . . .
between . . . different social levels, in their ranking of certain
occupations, these differences on the average do not appear to
be highly significant."[5]

With regard to the first conclusion, the present study attempts
to determine whether or not the Spokane respondents show a
variation with respect to their rankings of occupations in the

central and polar regions of the prestige hierarchy similar to that demonstrated by the English respondents.

Table 2, "Number of Respondents Ranking Each Occupation According to Prestige Level, in the Spokane Study," presents tabulations of the questionnaire data. The table reveals the rank order of each of the thirty occupations which resulted from the total number of respondents ranking each occupation as Very High, High, Average, Low, or Very Low. For purposes of analysis, it was necessary to assign weights to the five categories as follows: Very High, 1; High, 2; Average, 3; Low, 4; and Very Low, 5. The rank order of each of the occupations was determined by making use of these weights and taking the arithmetic mean of each frequency distribution. These means were then arranged in order from the lowest to the highest. Thus, in Table 2, the occupations at the top and bottom are those which were ranked as having the highest and lowest prestige, respectively.

It was decided that a determination of the standard deviation of each of the thirty frequency distributions would provide an adequate measure of the variability of the respondents with respect to the ranking of occupations in different sections of the prestige hierarchy. These standard deviations appear in the column on the extreme right of Table 2.

The second conclusion of Hall's and Jones's study with which this paper is concerned is the contention that there is a close correspondence between a pre-existing schema for the classification of occupations, the English Standard Classification (Table 3), and the empirical judgments of respondents as to the prestige of these occupations. Thus, one would expect a high correlation between the rankings of occupations in the standard classification utilized by Hall and Jones, and the arithmetic means of the rankings resulting from empirical research.

In Table 4, these means are presented for each occupation alongside that occupation's classification in the standard schema. The correlation of the arithmetic mean of the ranking by the English respondents, for each of the occupations, with the rankings in the English Standard Classification, results in a Pearsonian r of .978.

Whether or not a high correlation also exists between the ranks

TABLE 2—Number of Respondents Ranking Each Occupation According to Prestige Level, in the Spokane Study

Rank Order	Occupation	Very High No.	High No.	Average No.	Low No.	Very Low No.	Standard Deviation*
1	Medical Doctor	184	111	17	0	1	.63
2	Minister	180	99	31	2	1	.73
3	Lawyer	115	147	45	3	2	.76
4	Business Executive	68	191	50	3	1	.67
5	Certified Public Accountant	54	173	83	2	1	.74
6	Teacher (Elementary grades)	40	152	104	5	2	.72
7	Farmer (Large acreage)	28	155	125	3	0	.66
8	Plant Superintendent	46	172	94	0	0	.67
9	Office Manager	22	173	115	1	0	.60
10	Civil Servant	38	151	113	7	2	.74
11	News Reporter	27	116	156	11	1	.72
12	Electrician	18	95	194	5	0	.62
13	Insurance Agent	11	100	185	11	2	.64

No.	Occupation						
14	Carpenter	13	79	215	4	0	.53
15	Small Contractor	10	72	222	7	1	.53
16	Chief Cook (Hotel)	12	77	209	15	0	.61
17	Policeman	18	77	178	28	7	.78
18	Traveling Salesman	5	61	219	19	4	.60
19	Bricklayer	7	57	218	24	6	.64
20	Newsstand-Cigar Stand Manager	4	38	231	34	2	.52
21	Sales Clerk	8	24	241	36	2	.53
22	Tractor Driver (Agricultural)	13	22	225	50	2	.65
23	Routine Office Clerk	5	21	237	44	1	.51
24	Farm Laborer	15	26	182	80	8	.79
25	Delivery Man (Truck)	6	10	223	68	3	.50
26	Coal Miner	9	15	191	87	8	.70
27	Railway Porter	5	21	151	113	17	.76
28	Dock Laborer	5	9	156	120	16	.71
29	Bartender	4	9	144	91	44	.84
30	Street Cleaner	5	19	113	146	31	.81

* In computing standard deviations, the following weights were given to prestige levels: very high—1; high—2; average—3; low—4; very low—5.

TABLE 3—*The English Standard Classification*

Rank	Occupational Group
1	Professional and high administrative
2	Managerial and Executive
3	Inspectional, Supervisory and other non-manual, higher grade
4	Inspectional, Supervisory and other non-manual, lower grade
5	Skilled Manual and routine grades of non-manual
6	Semi-skilled Manual
7	Unskilled Manual

of occupations according to the English Standard Classification and the empirical judgments of the Spokane sample as to the prestige of these occupations, is one of the questions which the present study attempts to answer. The arithmetic means of the ranking of occupations by the Spokane respondents are also presented in Table 4. When these means are correlated with the English standard classificatory ranking of the same occupations, a Pearsonian r of .901 is obtained. This correlation can be used as an index of the degree to which an ordering of occupations by the English standard classificatory schema represents, for Spokane adults, a ranking of occupations with respect to their prestige or social standing.

Many class studies in the United States have made use of the Edwards Census Classification of occupations[6] for the definition of social classes. Thus, in addition to carrying out the above correlation, the six categories of occupations in the Edwards classification were correlated with the empirical rankings of occupations by Spokane respondents. This constituted a further test of Hall's and Jones's conclusion that a close correspondence can exist between a predetermined classification of occupations and the empirical ordering of these occupations by the population sampled. This calculation resulted in a Pearsonian r of .885.

The Spokane data concerned with a third conclusion of the English study, that there are no major differences between the English respondents belonging to different occupational groups as to their ranking of the thirty occupations, is found in Tables

5a and 5b. In Table 5a are presented the arithmetic means of the rankings of the thirty occupations by each of six occupational groups. These six groups are a result of classifying the respondents' replies as to their occupations, using the *Dictionary of Occupational Titles*.[7] The "Agricultural, Fishery and Forestry" category was omitted as the resulting N for that group was only 4. In addition, the subcategories under Skilled, Semi-skilled, and Unskilled occupations were combined. Thus, whereas the *Dictionary of Occupational Titles* contains ten occupational groups, only six were used in the present analysis.

The extent to which the members of the six occupational groups agree in their ranking of the thirty occupations can be measured by correlating the mean rankings by each occupational group with the mean rankings by every other occupational group. The resulting fifteen correlation coefficients are presented in Table 4.

Before any conclusions can be drawn concerning the applicability of the three generalizations made by Hall and Jones to the Spokane data, certain methodological limitations of the present study must be taken into account. The most important of these stems from the fact that, whereas the English respondents were asked to order the occupations from one to thirty, the American respondents were asked to rank each occupation on a five-point scale, from Very High to Very Low.

This limitation results in an additional difficulty. The method used by Hall and Jones of determining the arithmetic mean of the ranking by all respondents of each occupation, consisted of calculating the median judgment of each occupation for the four subdivisions (age groups) of each five occupational categories. The arithmetic mean of the twenty resulting medians was determined. If this method were carried out with the Spokane data, it would result in a large proportion of tied rankings, since the medians could only vary from one to five. Therefore, an alternative procedure for the calculation of arithmetic mean rankings was necessitated. This method consisted of a direct calculation of the arithmetic mean ranking by all respondents, for each occupation, taking into account the

TABLE 4—*Prestige Ranking of Occupations by all Respondents in the English Study and in the Spokane Study*

England					Spokane		
Rank Order	Occupation	Standard Classi-fication	A.M. of Ranking N-706	A.M. of Ranking N-312	Standard Classi-fication	Occupation	Rank Order
1	Medical Officer	1	1.3	1.48	1	Medical Doctor	1
2	Company Director	1	1.6	1.97	1	Business Executive	4
3	County Solicitor	1	2.6	1.81	1	Lawyer	3
4	Chartered Accountant	1	3.2	2.12	1	Certified Pub. Accountant	5
5	Civil Servant (Exec.)	2	6.0	2.40	2	Civil Servant (Exec.)	10
6	Business Manager	2	6.0	2.31	2	Office Manager	9
7	Works Manager	2	6.4	2.30	2	Plant Superintendent	8
8	Nonconformist Minister	2	6.4	1.49	2	Minister	2
9	Farmer (over 100 acres)	1	7.3	2.23	1	Farmer (large acreage)	7
10	Elem. School Teacher	3	10.8	2.18	3	Teacher (Elem. Grades)	6
11	Jobbing Master Building	3	11.4	2.73	3	Small Contractor	15
12	News Reporter	3	11.8	2.44	3	News Reporter	11

13	Commercial Traveler	3	12.0	2.86	3	Traveling Salesman	18
14	Chef	4	13.8	2.73	4	Chief Cook (Hotel)	16
15	Insurance Agent	4	14.6	2.66	4	Insurance Agent	13
16	Newsagent and Tobacconist	4	15.0	2.97	4	Newsstand-Cigar S. Mgr.	20
17	Policeman	5	16.1	2.76	5	Policeman	17
18	Routine Clerk	5	16.1	3.05	5	Routine Office Clerk	23
19	Fitter	5	17.6	2.60	5	Electrician	12
20	Carpenter	5	18.6	2.68	5	Carpenter	14
21	Shop Assistant	5	20.2	3.00	5	Sales Clerk	21
22	Bricklayer	5	20.2	2.89	5	Bricklayer	19
23	Tractor Driver (Agric.)	6	23.0	3.02	6	Tractor Driver (Agric.)	22
24	Coal Heaver	5	23.2	3.23	5	Coal Miner	26
25	Railway Porter	7	25.3	3.31	7	Railway Porter	27
26	Agricultural Labourer	6	25.5	3.12	6	Farm Labourer	24
27	Carter	6	25.8	3.17	6	Delivery Man (Truck)	25
28	Barman	7	26.4	3.53	7	Bartender	29
29	Dock Labourer	7	27.0	3.43	7	Dock Laborer	28
30	Road Sweeper	7	28.9	3.57	7	Street Cleaner	30

TABLE 5a—*Prestige Ranking of Occupations by Six Occupational Groups in the Spokane Study*

Rank order by all respondents	Occupation	Arithmetic Means of Rankings by Six Occupational Groups					
		Professional and Managerial (N = 68)	Clerical and Sales (N = 75)	Service (N = 46)	Skilled (N = 70)	Semi-Skilled (N = 30)	Un-Skilled (N = 19)
1	Medical Doctor	1.51	1.32	1.48	1.57	1.57	1.42
2	Minister	1.50	1.39	1.65	1.54	1.73	1.79
3	Lawyer	1.84	1.53	1.46	1.99	2.03	1.68
4	Business Executive	1.90	1.87	2.02	2.09	1.93	2.11
5	Certified Public Accountant	2.10	2.08	2.20	2.17	1.87	2.26
6	Teacher (Elem. Grades)	2.13	2.26	2.17	2.09	2.30	2.32
7	Farmer (large acreage)	2.44	2.29	2.24	2.30	2.30	2.42
8	Plant Superintendent	2.18	1.97	2.30	2.13	2.27	2.26
9	Office Manager	2.37	2.13	2.35	2.29	2.50	2.37
10	Civil Servant	2.29	2.29	2.33	2.29	2.29	2.42
11	News Reporter	2.37	2.49	2.52	2.51	2.50	2.84

12	Electrician	2.76	2.59	2.52	2.53	2.47	2.58
13	Insurance Agent	2.68	2.57	2.67	2.70	2.70	2.68
14	Carpenter	2.85	2.68	2.70	2.54	2.53	2.63
15	Small Contractor	2.81	2.80	2.72	2.67	2.60	2.63
16	Chief Cook (Hotel)	2.85	2.76	2.67	2.64	2.60	2.84
17	Policeman	2.76	2.73	2.64	2.77	2.83	2.94
18	Traveling Salesman	2.88	2.81	2.87	2.87	2.90	2.84
19	Bricklayer	3.10	2.99	2.85	2.66	2.26	2.95
20	Newsstand-Cigar Store Manager	2.98	2.97	2.96	2.99	2.93	3.00
21	Sales Clerk	3.07	2.97	2.96	2.89	2.97	3.42
22	Tractor Driver (Agric.)	3.13	3.15	2.96	2.93	2.87	2.95
23	Routine Office Clerk	3.12	3.15	2.89	2.93	3.03	3.26
24	Farm Laborer	3.32	3.25	2.83	3.04	3.07	3.05
25	Delivery Man (Truck)	3.30	3.28	3.13	3.01	3.00	3.32
26	Coal Miner	3.40	3.31	3.13	3.11	2.93	3.21
27	Railway Porter	3.54	3.54	3.26	3.30	3.10	3.72
28	Dock Laborer	3.61	3.53	3.38	3.26	3.28	3.50
29	Bartender	3.86	3.67	3.29	3.31	3.28	3.24
30	Street Cleaner	3.76	3.69	3.46	3.37	3.43	3.63

frequency distribution and the weights assigned to the five categories.

A further limitation to this study involves the justification for the assignation of weights to these five categories. Much of the present analysis rests on the assumption that respondents regard the difference between Very High and High categories, for example, as equal to the difference between High and Average categories. Actually, there exists no proof for the truth of this assumption. However, it seems reasonable to believe that, whether or not any given respondent conceives of the difference between two adjacent categories as being greater than that between two other adjacent categories, the variation with regard to these different conceptions among all respondents will be largely random. Thus, an analysis based on the responses of the entire sample should not be affected to any great extent on this account.

It is necessary to consider the fact that the responses of English males are being compared with those of both sexes in the Spokane sample. The lack of a detailed analysis of male and female respondents combined in the English study makes it difficult to compare the attitudes of both sexes from each country. In view of the fact that the English study found very little difference between male and female responses, however, it was deemed preferable to utilize the responses of Spokane females rather than to reduce the Spokane sample by approximately one-half.

Another fact which must be taken into account is the possibility that a number of occupations, although described in equivalent terminology for both countries, may not be identical in nature. Finally, the difficulties of generalizing from the representative sample of Spokane to the population of the United States, should be kept in mind.

In the light of these methodological limitations, it is now possible to consider the applicability of the three conclusions reached by Hall and Jones to the Spokane sample.

As for the first conclusion, upon inspection of the standard deviation in Table 2, there is no observable tendency for the standard deviations to be smaller for the occupations ranked at the poles of the prestige hierarchy. Assuming that this fact is not due to methodological differences between the two studies, the data supported the concusion that the Spokane respondents show no greater agreement on the prestige rankings of the polar occupations than they accord to occupations in the central region of the prestige hierarchy. It would be questionable to generalize the data on this point from the English and the Spokane studies to their respective countries. However, to the extent that this can be done, a hypothesis which may be tendered to explain the differences is that there exists a greater degree of mobility, in both the high and low-status occupations, in the United States than in England. This would account for a greater degree of disagreement in the United States as to the true status of a person engaging in an occupation generally accorded either high or low prestige.

With respect to Hall's and Jones's statement that there is a close correspondence between the ranks of occupations according to the English Standard Classification and the empirical prestige ranking of these occupations, the data indicate that this conclusion is applicable to the Spokane sample. This is in view of the fact that there is a Pearsonian r of .901 between the empirical ratings by the Spokane sample and the occupational rankings according to the English Standard Classification. Using the z test of differences between r's, however, we find that there is a statistically significant difference at approximately the 1 per cent level between this correlation coefficient and Hall's and Jones's r of .978. Thus, although the ranking of occupations in the English Standard Classification correlates to a high degree with the empirical ranking by the Spokane sample, this correlation is statistically significantly less than the correlation involving the English data.

It is interesting to note that the three skilled-labor occupations, electrician, carpenter and bricklayer, were ranked higher in the prestige hierarchy by the Spokane respondents than was true of the English respondents, i.e., electrician, Spokane, 12, England, 19; carpenter, Spokane, 14, England, 20; bricklayer, Spokane, 19, England, 22.

Concerning the conclusion of Hall and Jones that the differences in the rankings of occupations by various occupational groups are small, the data in Table 5b lends support to the generalization of this conclusion to the Spokane sample. The fact that the fifteen correlation coefficients in Table 5b are all above .940 indicates that the judgments of the different occupational groups as to the prestige of occupations correlate very highly with one another.

Accumulation of data from cross-cultural studies may provide the basis for further analysis of hypotheses and theories concerning the relationship between occupation and prestige, as well as throw light upon related problems of social structure and organization.

TABLE 5b—*Correlation of the Mean Rankings of Occupations by the Six Occupational Groups in the Spokane Study*

Occupational Groups	Pearsonian Coefficient of Correlation
Professional and Managerial: Clerical and Sales	.991
Professional and Managerial: Service	.964
Professional and Managerial: Skilled	.980
Professional and Managerial: Semi-skilled	.963
Professional and Managerial: Unskilled	.940
Clerical and Sales: Service	.979
Clerical and Sales: Skilled	.980
Clerical and Sales: Semi-skilled	.961
Clerical and Sales: Unskilled	.958
Service: Skilled	.964
Service: Semi-skilled	.951
Service: Unskilled	.965
Skilled: Semi-skilled	.974
Skilled: Unskilled	.955
Semi-skilled: Unskilled	.945

CONCEPTIONS OF THE CLASS STRUCTURE AS REVEALED BY SAMPLES OF ENGLISH AND AMERICAN BOYS*

It is generally recognized that systems of stratification and conceptions of these systems vary from one society to another. A system of stratification is intimately linked to the level and type of integration existing in a particular society.[8] In the historical-cultural growth of nations there develop differential complexes of basic values, cultural themes, and national myths which provide the basis for societal integration and determine the kind of social-status system which functions as an integral part of the organic whole.

Pfautz, after a review of the current literature on social stratification, points to the need for empirical studies relating social-status systems to social systems generally.[9] Comparative studies offer one approach to the problem. The relation of a social-status system to the larger society is, of course, more easily recognized in comparative research dealing with the more distinct systems of stratification, such as caste, estate, and class arrangements. Studies of two-class societies can hardly be expected to delineate distinctions as sharp as might be anticipated from the comparative study of a caste and a class society. An analysis of two class-societies may, however, be of value. As

---

* From *Research Studies* (Washington State University), Vol. XXII, June, 1954.

Lerner has pointed out: ". . . it remains true that nations are realities, that their cultures develop along different lines and in different ways, and that the world inside the heads of their people is a characteristic world."[10]

The United States and England, as pointed out in the introduction to this monograph, share much of the western European religious-political-economic heritage. They have a common language; they are both nominally Christian countries with a representative form of government; they subscribe to similar conceptions of civil liberties, individual freedom, and equality before the law; they share in large part the same literature and modes of artistic expression. But the institutionalization of these ways of life has proceeded differently in each country.

England and the United States are both class societies. Their respective systems of stratification have, however, developed in relation to quite different historical situations, and it may be assumed not only that the two status systems as they are integrated with the larger societies are different from each other, but also that they are conceptualized by the respective populations in somewhat different fashions.

The analysis which follows is a description of the differences and similarities revealed in the responses of a group of American boys and a group of English boys to questions concerning the nature of the system of social stratification in their respective countries. It is believed that this analysis holds implications for theory with reference to the relationship of status systems to the general social organization of a society.

The data upon which the study is based were collected by means of a questionnaire administered to a sample of thirteen- and fourteen-year-old school boys in London and to similar groups of boys in Seattle and Spokane. Neither sample was random, but both were purposeful in the sense that the selection of schools was made with a knowledge of the ecology of the cities and the general socio-economic characteristics of the various school populations.

The London sample consisted of 600 boys. The Seattle-Spokane sample numbered 744. Both samples responded to the same questions.* The analysis presented here is of the responses to questions dealing most directly with social class. The English and United States samples are referred to as nationality groups. Each nationality group was divided into three social-class groups on the basis of the prestige of the occupations of the boys' fathers.† The six resulting groupings lend themselves to analysis either by nationality or by social class. Responses to selected items on the questionnaire were tabulated in number and per cent for each of the six groups by nationality and social class.

The major analysis presented here is limited to a consideration of the differences between the two nationality groups. Class differences will be pointed out only when they seem to be particularly pertinent. The discussion is in terms of percentage distributions.‡

Early in the questionnaire, the two nationality groups were asked: "Do you think that there are social classes in the United States (England)?" Three alternative response categories were provided: "1. I do not understand the question; 2. Yes; 3. No."

Forty-five per cent of the U.S. sample and 29.6 per cent of the English sample indicated that they thought social classes existed in their respective countries. Approximately 10 per cent of each nationality group thought that they did not exist, leaving 43.4 per cent of the U.S. group and 59.0 per cent of the English sample indicating that they did not understand the question. The U.S. sample appeared to be more conscious of social class than were the English boys. These responses may be a reflection

---

* Slight changes in wording were necessary to insure comprehension by American boys.

† A correlation of .89 was found between the prestige ranking represented by the Edwards Census Classification and those of the English Standard Classification. This permitted equating certain occupational categories of the two classifications and thus coding both samples by a slightly modified Edwards Classification. See U.S. Bureau of the Census, *Population: Comparative Statistics for the United States, 1870-1940* (Washington: Government Printing Office, 1943), pp. 176-79.

The number in each status group was as follows: English I (upper) 89; English II, 349; English III, 162; U.S. I, 242; U.S. II, 320; U.S. III, 182.

‡ No statistical test of significance of differences between percentages is used in this analysis inasmuch as it is felt that the samples do not meet the assumptions of such tests.

of lack of familiarity with the term "social class" rather than a lack of wider cognizance of status differences in the respective societies. Analysis of this question by social class and nationality reveals that the highest percentage responding in the affirmative—believing that social classes exist—was found in U.S. II (49.1). Approximately 45 per cent of both U.S. and English I answered "Yes." U.S. III had the next highest percentage recognizing social classes, leaving English II and III the least conscious of them.

We were interested not only in seeing how wide was the recognition of social classes in each nationality group, but also in obtaining some idea of the terms in which the respondents thought about social classes. The succeeding question asked those who had said that they believed classes existed to write "the names you would give to the social classes." The questionnaire gave no indication of the number of classes to be named. In coding the responses, however, provision was made for four levels: roughly, upper, upper middle, middle, and lower.

By inspection of a sample of responses, six basic criteria categories were formed: (1) *Hierarchical*—upper, middle, lower, etc.; (2) *Work*—working, don't have to work, leisure class, won't work, do most of the work, etc.; (3) *Money*—rich, poor, not rich-not poor, etc.; (4) *Political*—Conservative, Liberal, Labour Party, Republican, Democrat, Socialist, etc.; (5) *"Social"* —royalty, peerage, posh, upper set, society set, common, live in slums; (6) *Occupational*—professionals, have best jobs, have poor jobs, etc.

Less than 6 per cent of each nationality group designated four or more classes, and in these cases it was nearly always true that the names they gave to the "upper-middle" class were in the same category as were their designations for the "middle" class. Therefore, in the comments which follow, only three levels will be considered.

Table 6 shows that the names given to the social classes by the two nationality groups were rather consistently drawn from different criteria categories. National differences were greater in this respect than were the differences between social classes.

The money criterion category was most frequently used by all

TABLE 6—Criteria Categories Used in Naming the Social Classes, by Nationality Group and Social Class*

Nationality and Class	Upper Level		Middle Level		Lower Level	
	Category	Per Cent	Category	Per Cent	Category	Per Cent
U.S. I (N = 242)	Money	18.2	Hierarchical	30.2	Money	17.8
U.S. II (N = 320)	Money	20.0	Hierarchical	27.8	Money	19.7
U.S. III (N = 182)	Money	12.1	Hierarchical	20.3	Money	11.0
Eng. I (N = 89)	Hierarchical	23.6	Hierarchical	37.1	Hierarchical	18.0
Eng. II (N = 349)	Hierarchical	11.5	Hierarchical	20.3	Work	9.2
Eng. III (N = 162)	Hierarchical	4.3	Hierarchical	8.6	Work	3.7

* Modal categories used are exclusive of "no answer" and "unclassified" responses. Roughly 50 to 75 per cent of the responses fell into these two categories.

the U.S. social classes in naming the "upper" and "lower" levels; the "middle" level was most frequently called "middle," which was coded as hierarchical; however, in this context "middle" may have meant "not rich—not poor."

Names from the money criterion category were not frequently used by any English social class. English I employed hierarchical designations for each of the three levels; English II and III used hierarchical names for the "upper" and "middle" levels and work ("working") for the "lower" level.

After the respondents had had the opportunity to name the classes, they were asked to name the class "to which you and your family belong." Most of each social-class group in both countries omitted this question. Nearly all of the U.S. sample responding to the question identified themselves with the middle class in hierarchical terms. This was also true of the English group, although small percentages of both English II and III identified themselves with political parties.

Much later in the questionnaire—on the second day of its administration, in fact—the respondents were asked to complete these sentences: "Upper class people are those who . . .; middle class people are those who . . .; working class people are those who. . . ."

Responses to these open-ended questions revealed that both nationality groups were probably thinking about the same kinds of people when they had earlier given them different names. The upper class is most frequently described by both nationality groups and by all social classes as: "are rich," "have lots of money," or "can buy everything they want." The second most frequently mentioned descriptions of the upper level revealed differences by nationality; all U.S. social classes characterized it in terms of high occupations, and all English social classes described it in terms of snobbery. Snobbery did not enter the descriptions of the upper level by the U.S. sample nearly so frequently. It was the fifth most frequent characterization by U.S. III, eighth by U.S. II, and fifteenth in descriptions by U.S. I.

People in the middle class were also most frequently described in terms of money—"have some money," "not rich—not poor," "comfortably off"—by both nationality groups and by all social classes. The second most frequent description tended to be by occupation in both nationality groups.

The lower level was described by both nationality groups and all social classes in terms of work—"work hard for a living," "work hard for little pay," etc. The second most frequent characterization of the lower class tended to be in terms of money—"the poor," "haven't much money," etc.—with one interesting exception: U.S. III described themselves as "ordinary people with ordinary or average jobs."

It is evident that the two nationality groups, generally speaking, describe the people whom they believe to compose the three classes in quite similar terms, but at the same time they tend to give them different names. Both samples described the upper and lower levels in the same terms—money and work, respectively. But in the names they choose for them, the U.S. group stays consistently with the "money" criterion for the upper level and calls it rich; it forgets the "work" description of the lower level and calls it "poor"; whereas the English sample deviates from its description in the opposite manner, forgetting the "wealth" description and calling the upper level "upper class," while staying with "work" designation for the lower level.

Possibly the names are not important. However, one might hypothesize that wealth is more consistently translated into high social prestige—"upper class," with connotations of snobbery—in England than in the United States; hence the designation "Hierarchical." In the United States social prestige may not be so certain or so traditional a correlate of wealth. The most important thing about the rich in the United States is that they are rich, so they are called "rich."

"Working class" likewise has rather definite and widely accepted status and political connotations in England which are not present, at least in the same degree, in the United States. This may explain why a larger per cent of English III identified themselves with the working class (or the Labour Party) than was true of U.S. III; and it may also account for the consistency of the English groups in using the "work" criterion in describing the lower level as well as in designating it as "working class."

It does not help to explain the inconsistency of the U.S. sample in this respect.

In the area of the study concerned with mobility, we tried not only to obtain some idea of the respondents' attitudes toward upward mobility but also to get an indication as to what factors were thought to be important in "moving up in the world."

In approaching the first objective, nine questions* were selected on the basis of their pertinence to general conceptions not only as to the possibility of upward mobility but also concerning the "rightness" of trying to change one's social status. As indicated in the footnote, most of these questions were of the five-category response type: Strongly agree, agree, uncertain, disagree, and strongly disagree. When the "uncertain" and "no response"† categories were omitted, the two positive categories combined, we find that roughly 40 to 60 per cent of both nationality groups indicated by their responses to the various questions that they did not wish to accept the status to which they were born. The U.S. group was more apt to consider movement "right and proper," and they evidenced more general acceptance of mobility as a goal than did the English sample. For example, responses to the question, "We are all born to our social positions and it would not do to change them," revealed that only 17.3 per cent of the U.S. sample accepted this statement, 53.5 per cent disagreeing, as compared with 30.1 per cent of the English group accepting and 38 per cent disagreeing.

---

* Do you think you have as good a chance as other boys of moving up in the world? (As good, better, poorer); Do you think you have as good a chance as your father to move up in the world? (As good, better, poorer); The world is full of opportunities open to everyone. (Strongly agree, uncertain, disagree, strongly disagree); Most boys should try to get a better job than their fathers had. (Same); It is wrong for a person to be dissatisfied with his position in life. (Same); If a person doesn't do better than his father did, he is no good. (Same); A person who is content with what he has will have a better life than one who is always trying to improve his position. (Same); The way to be happy in life is to be satisfied with whatever you have. (Same); We are all born to our various social positions and it would not do to change them. (Same).

† The "no response" category seldom contained more than 1 or 2 per cent of a social class.

A much larger percentage of the English sample than of the U.S. sample also agreed to the statement: "It's wrong for a person to be dissatisfied with his position in life" (English, 41.6 per cent; U.S., 28.0 per cent).

However, the responses to more concrete questions, such as "Most boys should try to get a better job than their fathers," showed a larger percentage of the English boys to be in agreement than was true of the U.S. group (59.0 and 40.6 per cent, respectively). Neither nationality group would go so far as to agree that "if a person doesn't do better than his father, he is no good." Eighty-three per cent of the U.S. group and 75 per cent of the English sample disagreed with this statement.

Analysis of the remaining five questions in this area did not reveal any very meaningful national differences. It is significant that the responses of the two nationality groups were almost identical with respect to the question: "Do you think that you have as good a chance as your father had of moving up in the world?" This was a three-category response question, and the results were as follows: "Better"—U.S., 54.2 per cent, English, 54.9; "as good"—U.S. 39.5 per cent, English 41.1; "poorer"—U.S., 3.4 per cent, English, 2.8.

Social-class differences in attitude toward mobility were evident. The analysis not being complete in this area, only general statements can be made. It appears that both U.S. and English III are more inclined to accept their status than are the two upper levels, and are also less optimistic about their chances for upward mobility. U.S. and English II are the most interested in upward mobility and are the most optimistic. These class differences were somewhat greater in England than in the United States.

Table 7 presents the most frequently mentioned factors thought to be first, second, or third in importance in moving up in the world, by nationality group and by social class.

It will be noted that different factors were selected by the two nationality groups as being of *first* importance in upward mobility. All three social-class groups in the United States designated "education" most frequently, whereas all three social classes in the English sample were most apt to think "hard work"

TABLE 7—*Factors Thought to be First, Second, and Third in Importance in Upward Mobility, by Nationality Group and Social Class**

Nationality and Class	First in Importance Factor	Per Cent	Second in Importance Factor	Per Cent	Third in Importance Factor	Per Cent
U.S. I (N = 242)	Education	24.0	Good Character	21.5	Non-aggressive personality traits	17.4
U.S. II (N = 320)	Education	25.3	Hard Work Non-aggressive personality traits	15.9 15.9	Non-aggressive personality traits	15.6
U.S. III (N = 182)	Education	25.8	Hard Work	15.4	Good Character	17.0
Eng. I (N = 89)	Education Hard Work	21.3 21.3	Hard Work Intelligence	19.1 19.1	Non-aggressive personality traits	15.7
Eng. II (N = 349)	Hard Work	17.5	Non-aggressive personality traits	13.5	Non-aggressive personality traits	15.8
Eng. III (N = 162)	Hard Work	18.5	Good Character	13.0	Non-aggressive personality traits	14.8

* Modal categories used are exclusive of "no answer" and "unclassified" responses. Roughly 2 to 15 per cent of the responses fell into these two categories.

to be of first importance. However, "education" was mentioned as frequently as was "hard work" by English I.

The results as to the second most important factor in upward mobility were not so clear-cut, either by nationality group or social class. "Non-aggressive personality traits," "good character," and "hard work" were most frequently mentioned; however, "non-aggressive personality traits" were ranked third by all social-class groups in both national samples except English III, where responses were most frequently in the related category "good character."

Also determined was the rank order of factors thought to be first, second, or third in importance in upward mobility, by nationality group and social class. Comment on this rank order will be confined to a few observations. The factor second most frequently mentioned as being of first importance by the U.S. sample was "hard work" for U.S. I and III, and "non-aggressive personality traits" for U.S. II. The English sample reversed the two, listing "education" most frequently after "hard work." Also, it is interesting to note the rank of the factors of "intelligence" and "good character" in the two nationality samples. "Intelligence" was the third most frequently listed factor of most importance in upward mobility by all social classes in the English sample, but was the fifth in frequency in the U.S. sample. "Good character" was third in the U.S. sample and fourth in the English group.

The two nationality groups thus designated the same factors as being important in upward mobility. The difference between them lies in the order of importance imputed to the various factors. Generally speaking, "education" is ranked above "hard work" by the U.S. sample, and vice versa for the English group. "Good character" is ranked above "intelligence" by the U.S. sample and vice versa in the case of English boys.

The attitudes of the two nationality groups toward mobility may be summarized as follows: The English group showed more acceptance of the social-class status to which they were born than did the U.S. group. At the same time, however, they evidenced more interest than did the U.S. sample in getting a better job than their fathers had. This might be interpreted as a tendency to limit mobility, in the thinking of the English boys, to occupational improvement within the generally accepted social-class structure.

No attempt will be made to interpret the findings relative to what was thought to be the most important factor in mobility other than to indicate that in the American case the emphasis upon "education," "hard work," and "good character," in that order, is in keeping with the "American Creed," while the English responses seem to reflect English institutions which have placed less emphasis on universal free education, have tended to put a premium on "hard work" and "intelligence," and are probably somewhat less moralistic in general orientation. It may be pointed out that although both societies are class societies, our data revealed that the social classes are apt to be given different names and that they are conceptualized in somewhat different ways by the two nationality groups. Likewise, attitudes toward mobility appear to be different, and although the same factors are thought to be important in upward mobility they are arranged in a different order of importance by the two samples. These differences, as has been indicated, are thought to be related to broad, cultural, historically derived differences in basic values and to the ways in which these values have been institutionalized in the two countries.

chapter fifteen

A CROSS-NATIONAL STUDY OF
ATTITUDES BY SOCIAL CLASS*

A comparatively recent development in the general area of culture of personality has become known as the national character school.[11] Many of the national character studies of modern societies have been made "at a distance" and have been criticized, not only as to methodology, but also in relation to basic assumptions.†

Studies of contemporary nations have been criticized for apparently assuming greater cultural homogeneity than may actually exist.[12] The basic uniformities in culture patterns which these studies postulate have been related to "basic personality structure" which is thought to cut across status, class, and other subcultural units. Mead, Bateson, and Gorer all recognize status or social-class differences in a culture in relation to personality. They tend, however, to see them either as "versions of" or "systematically related to" the wider cultural pattern. Linton, on the other hand, in discussing status-personality, says: ". . . the members of each class are shaped by *their own culture* and their personality norms derive first of all from this culture and only secondarily from the culture of the larger configurations of which their class forms a part." Later, however, he suggests that ". . . we cannot dismiss the possibility that Status Personalities are really cultural fictions."[13] J. H. Steward stated the basic problem in the form of a question to his colleagues: "One

---

* From *Research Studies*, Washington State University, Vol. XXIV, No. 3, 1956.

† A brief critique of national character was presented in Part I of this monograph.

question that always bothered me is whether the national uniformities . . . are relatively greater than the subcultural differences between segments of a population; and that, it would seem, is a purely empirical thing to be determined before anything else." His question was not answered.[14]

Margaret Mead, in the paper cited above, has distinguished between the related fields of culture and personality studies, national character, and attitude studies. The present chapter is not a national character study; no attempt is made to show patterned responses, or recurrent cultural themes, much less to discover basic personality structures. But as a brief analysis of attitudes in relation to social class and nationality, it is nevertheless relevant to the question of national homogeneity and is confined to the implications of the assumption of such a high degree of cultural homogeneity as to slight the influence of social-class differences.

The data upon which this study is based were collected by a questionnaire administered to a sample of thirteen- and fourteen-year-old school boys[15] in London, England, and to a similar group of male students in Seattle and Spokane, Washington. Neither sample was random, but made with a knowledge of the ecology of the cities and the general socio-economic character-istics of the various school populations. The London sample consisted of 600 boys. The Seattle-Spokane sample numbered 744. Both samples responded to 210 items which were later formed into twenty-two "attitudinal areas" of from three to twenty-five items each. The selection of items was based upon their pertinence to the previously designated categories.

The English and U.S. samples are referred to as nationality groups. Each nationality group was divided into three social-class groups on the basis of the prestige of the occupations of the boys' fathers. A correlation of .89 was found between prestige ranking represented by the Edwards Census Classification and those of the English Standard Classification.[16] This permitted equating certain occupational categories of the two classifications and thus coding both samples by a slightly modified Edwards Classification. The six resulting groupings lend themselves to analysis either by nationality or by social class. The number in each status group is as follows: English I (upper), 89; English II, 349; English III, 162; U.S. I, 242; U.S. II, 320; U.S. III, 182. Responses to selected items on the questionnaire were tabulated in number and per cent for each of the six groups by nationality and social class.*

As a means of determining the relative homogeneity of the groups by nationality as compared with social class in reference to each attitudinal area, the accumulated per cent of responses from the modal response category toward the positive extreme was obtained for each item. (The modal category was included or excluded, depending upon which procedure brought the accumulated total nearest to 50 per cent.) The median ranking of the six groups on all items in an area was then computed. Thus the responses of each of the six groups were ranked in reference to each attitudinal area.

In order to compare rankings by nationality and social class, the mean difference between rankings by nationality, English I, II, III, and U.S. I, II, III, was computed and compared with the mean difference in ranking by social classes, English and U.S. I, English and U.S. II, English and U.S. III. These mean differences are employed in summarizing the social class and national differences by attitudinal areas in Table 8. In this ranking process one may have a partial test of the hypothesis of high national homogeneity. If all responses should rank by nationality, that is, all English social-class groups ranking high and all U.S. social-class groups ranking low, or vice versa, the differences would be clearly in terms of nationality and would imply national homogeneity. If all should rank by social-class groups, that is, the same social-class group responses having the same or similar rank in each country, the differences would be between classes, implying cross-national social-class similarity.

The data did not rank in such a clear-cut fashion. Responses in thirteen attitudinal areas ranked by nationality; in the re-

* Here we encounter the problem which the national character students have pointed out. The concept of social class is a part of a national culture. The difficulty of holding social class constant on the one hand, and nationality on the other is, of course, recognized.

maining nine areas, by social class. The thirteen areas in which national differences were found to be greater than social class differences are: (1) general status consciousness; (2) consciousness of status symbols; (3) respect for property; (4) receptiveness to authority; (5) attitude toward competition; (6) political attitudes; (7) tolerance for deviant behavior; (8) self-conception—general; (9) extrovertism; (10) importance of habits and manners; (11) conformity to peer groups; (12) conformity to the home; and (13) sibling relationships. A brief comment on

TABLE 8—*Mean Difference in Median Rank of the Six Groups by Nationality and Social Class in Reference to Each of the Attitudinal Areas*

Areas That Ranked by Nationality	National Differences*	Social-Class Differences*
1. Status Consciousness	1	0
2. Consciousness of Status Symbols	3	0
3. Attitude toward Property	3	1
4. Attitude toward Authority	2	1
5. Attitude toward Competition	2	1
6. Political Attitudes	3	1
7. Tolerance for Deviant Behavior	2	1
8. Self-Conception—General	2	1
9. Extrovertism	2	0
10. Personal Habits and Manners	3	1
11. Conformity in the Home	2	1
12. Conformity to Peer Groups	2	0
13. Sibling Relationships	1	1

Areas That Ranked by Social Class	National Differences*	Social-Class Differences*
1. Self-Conception—Will Power	0	1
2. Attitude toward Mobility	0	1
3. General Family Relationships	0	2
4. Parent-Child Relationships	1	2
5. Attitude toward Punishment	0	1
6. Personal Aggressiveness and Initiative	0	1
7. Attitude toward Force	0	2
8. Conformity in the School	0	1
9. Conception of the World	0	2

*Fractions adjusted to the nearest whole number.

the relative differences in each of these areas follows, although no attempt is made here to analyze how these attitudes "hold together" in relation to nationality. Research in national character has given consideration to most of them.

Responses to items in the general area of *status consciousness* revealed the English group to be more status-conscious than the U.S. sample. English III was the most status-conscious social-class group; U.S. I and U.S. III the least status-conscious.

In reference to another set of items dealing more specifically with *status symbols*, the rankings by nationalities were even more clear-cut. All English social-class groups ranked higher than any U.S. social-class group. English II and III ranked the highest; U.S. II and III ranked the lowest, with the upper social-class groups in both countries falling in between.

Responses to items in the area concerned with *respect for property* also showed that all English social-class groups ranked higher than any U.S. social-class group. English II and III had the greatest respect for property; U.S. I and II, the least.

As to the two nationality groups' belief in and *respect for authority*, the U.S. sample ranked the higher, with U.S. I and II showing more respect than U.S. III. English I ranked with U.S. III; English II and III were the least responsive to authority of the six social-class groups.

Responses to items dealing with *competition* revealed that the English group was more receptive to competition both in interpersonal relations and as a social force, than the U.S. sample. English I and II ranked the highest, U.S. I and III the lowest.

In the area of *political attitudes*, all English social-class groups ranked above all U.S. social-class groups, indicating that the English national sample expressed more democratic-liberal attitudes than did the U.S. sample. English III ranked the highest, followed by English II and I in that order. U.S. I ranked the lowest, with U.S. II and III tied—both lower than English I.

The English sample indicated that it was more *tolerant of deviant behavior* than was the U.S. sample. The items in this area did not deal with delinquent or criminal behavior, but rather with religion, sex, smoking, race, etc. English II ranked the highest and U.S. II the lowest in tolerance. All English social-class groups ranked above any U.S. social-class group.

Two sets of items attempted to reveal *self-conceptions*. The first dealt with conceptions of the self in a variety of interpersonal situations. In this area all English social-class groups ranked higher than any U.S. social-class group. The strongest conception of the self was found to exist in English II; the weakest in U.S. III. The second set of items was concerned only with "will power" in controlling emotions and appetites. These items were ranked by social class and are discussed later.

In the area dealing with *extroverted behavior*, i.e., boasting, showing off, etc., all U.S. social-class groups ranked above any English social-class group. U.S. III evidenced the greatest tendency toward extroverted behavior; English I and III the least.

The responses of the two nationality groups to items in the area of *personal habits and manners* indicated that all social-class groups in the English sample ranked above any social-class group in the U.S. sample. English III evidenced the most concern about personal habits and manners, and U.S. II the least.

Conformity was approached in three areas: in the home, to peer groups, and in the school. In the last, conformity to the school, differences among the social-class groups were found to be greater than the differences between the nationality groups and are discussed later. In the area of conformity in the home, the U.S. sample ranked higher than the English sample, with U.S. I and II ranking the highest in that order, followed by U.S. III and English III. English I and II revealed the least conformity in the home. Conformity to peer groups, however, was found to be stronger in the English sample, with no difference between social-class groups, all ranking above any U.S. social-class group. U.S. II showed the least conformity to peer groups.

The last of the thirteen areas in which responses to items indicated that national differences were greater than social-class differences was attitudes toward *sibling relationships*. National differences were not great, but the U.S. sample evidenced more satisfaction in this area than did the English group. U.S. II ranked the highest and English III the lowest.

In the nine remaining attitudinal areas, the responses of both the English and U.S. samples tended to rank by social-class groups rather than by nationality groups. These areas are: (1) self-conception—will power; (2) belief in and aspirations for upward mobility; (3) satisfaction with general family relationships; (4) satisfaction with parent-child relationships; (5) attitudes toward punishment; (6) attitudes toward personal aggressiveness; (7) attitudes toward force; (8) conformity in the school; and (9) conception of the world. Space does not permit consideration of the special nature of these attitudes as related to social class. Research in stratification indicates that a special relationship may exist.

Social-class group II, ranking the same in both countries, evidenced the highest conception of *will power* in controlling emotions and appetites. U.S. I and III ranked the same. English III ranked below English I and lowest of the six social-class groups.

With reference to the belief in the "rightness" of *mobility* and aspirations for upward mobility, responses to the items indicated that social-class group I evidenced the most interest in mobility, whereas II and III showed the least. U.S. III ranked the lowest of the six social-class groups.

Greatest satisfaction with *general family relationships* was shown by social-class group I; II and III evidenced less satisfaction, with English III ranking the lowest. In the more specific area *child-parent relationships*, the rankings by social-class groups were similar to those in the more general area: I revealing the greatest satisfaction—both national groups ranking the same—and II and III ranking lower, with English III lowest.

The items concerned with *punishment* were such as to give an indication of the severity of punishment thought to be appropriate to a large variety of acts. Social-class groups I and II were the most punitive, English II ranking the highest.

With reference to *personal aggressiveness and initiative*, social-class group I ranked the highest and III the lowest—the same in each country. However, English II showed more personal aggressiveness and initiative than did U.S. II.

Social-class group III evidenced the widest *acceptance of force*, both in response to personal and impersonal items. There was no difference in rank between U.S. I and II. However, English I ranked lower than English II and indeed lower than U.S. I and II.

Conformity in school was found to be somewhat higher in social-class group II than in I or III. However, U.S. III ranked as high as U.S. and English II.

In the area called *conception of the world*, social-class group III—ranking the same in both countries—evidenced a much more pessimistic outlook than did I and II. U.S. I was the most optimistic.

As was mentioned in the early paragraphs of this chapter, there is a tendency for some social scientists in their study of personality, and more particularly in the frame of reference of national character, to assume such a high degree of national homogeneity of culture as to justify general statements concerning "the personality of Americans," "the British character," and the like. A better understanding of the similarities and differences in basic personality characteristics existing between modern peoples is highly desirable, but such an understanding cannot be achieved by ignoring the discontinuities of social class. The social-class culture in modern societies may provide the primary cultural experiences in the formation of personality.

Of course a wide measure of national homogeneity can be assumed, as is indicated in this study by the finding that in thirteen of the twenty-two attitudinal areas the differences between the two nationality groups were greater than the differences among the social-class groups. However, the finding that social-class differences were greater than national differences in the nine remaining areas of attitudes indicates a significant degree of class similarity cutting across national lines. Attitudes in these nine areas have been shown by other research to be important in character formation.[17] Therefore, assumption of a high degree of homogeneity of culture that tends to ignore social class in relation to basic personality structure and national character in modern industrial societies would seem to be hazardous, if not unjustified.

chapter sixteen

PREDICTION OF ATTITUDES FROM
A KNOWLEDGE OF SOCIAL CLASS*

To determine the extent to which social class can be used as a predictor of certain attitudes of adolescent boys in England and in the United States, Guttman's prediction technique based on the "principle of maximum probability" was used. Assuming that the distribution of a given attribute in a population is known, the best method of predicting whether or not a given individual has that attribute is the method that will yield the least amount of error for the population as a whole. This method is to predict the modal category of the attribute or the category of a variable which has the highest frequency. The modal category minimizes the errors of prediction, as defined by the principle of maximum probability.

If a second variable, which divides the population into strata enables the number of errors made in the original prediction to be decreased, then predictive efficiency is increased. The extent of this increase in efficiency can be measured by the "coefficient of relative predictability," which compares the number of errors of prediction that would be made if the second variable were not used with the number of errors made by using the second variable. The formula for this coefficient is as follows:

$$C = \frac{E_2 - E_1}{E_2}$$

C = the coefficient of relative predictability.

E_1 = the proportion of predictions of attitude categories, from

---

* From "A Cross-national Study of the Prediction of Attitudes from Social Class" by Bernard Phillips (Pustilnik), unpublished Master's thesis, Washington State University, 1953. Published with the author's permission.

knowledge of the social class and the modal attitude for each class, that are errors.

E_2 = the proportion of predictions of attitude categories, without using social class but using the modal attitude of the total population, that are errors.

The limits of C are zero and one. If $E_1 = E_2$, then $C = 0$, and the predictor is of no aid. If $E_1 = 0$, then $C = 1$, and the predictor yields perfect prediction.

Social class is the predictor, and attitudes as expressed in answers to the questions are the variables to be predicted. C, therefore, is a measure of the extent to which the errors of prediction are reduced through using social class compared with the use of the modal attitude in the population.

The above method was supplemented by a prediction technique formulated by J. A. Jahn.[18] Like the above method it results in a coefficient which is a measure of the predictive efficiency of the rule for prediction used, and the coefficients for the two samples, on a given question, can be compared to determine whether or not social class is a better predictor for one sample than for the other. The difference between the two methods is that they involve different conditions for prediction. The principle of maximum probability has, as a condition for prediction, the determination of the best possible estimate of the variable to be predicted. This involves picking the modal category for each stratum of the population formed by the predictor. The supplementary method has as a condition for prediction an *a priori* rule stating the relation between the predictor and the variable to be predicted. For example, in the area of political attitudes the rule for prediction might be stated as follows: the upper social class will be most conservative, the middle class next most conservative, and the lower social class will be least conservative. This is not necessarily the best rule for prediction, as opposed to the method based on the principle of maximum probability. The formula used in this second technique is as follows:

$$C' = \frac{E_4 - E_3}{E_4}$$

C' = The coefficient of predictive efficiency.

E_3 = the observed proportion of predictions of attitude categories from knowledge of social class, and using the *a priori* rule for prediction, that are errors.

E_4 = the expected proportion of prediction of attitude categories from knowledge of the social class and the rule for prediction, assuming that the attitude variable is completely independent of social class, that are errors.

When $E_3 = E_4$, $C' = 0$, i.e., the rule for prediction yields the same number of errors as would be made by assuming that the predictor and the variable to be predicted are completely independent. When $E_3 = 0$, $C' = 1$, and the rule for prediction yields no errors of prediction. When E_3 is greater than E_4, C' becomes a negative number, and the rule for prediction results in more errors than would be made by assuming that the predictor and the variable to be predicted are completely independent. C' becomes, for the present study, a measure of the extent to which the *a priori* rule for the prediction of attitudes results in proportionately greater or fewer errors than would occur if the predictor (social class) and the variable to be predicted were completely independent.

In the questions analyzed in this study there were five possible answers to choose from, thus providing a range for the intensity of the attitudes. The variable to be predicted contains five categories while the predictor (social class) has only three categories. The two extra categories in the variable to be predicted, assuming they are not empty, prevent the possibility of perfect prediction in calculating either C or C'. Therefore, categories of the variable to be predicted were combined so that only three categories remained. This insures that the upper limit of C or C' is plus one, for either rule for prediction which is used. Adjacent categories were combined so as to equalize, as far as possible, the marginal distributions for the social classes and for the attitude variable. This was done, since perfect prediction is only possible if the marginal distributions of the predicted and predicting variables are equal, assuming none of the categories is empty.

Each attitude area was measured by from three to five questions; for a given class that attitude category was predicted which was modal to it for the greatest number of questions. For example, in the area of political attitudes the modal category for the responses of the American upper-class sample is found in the category indicating the greatest degree of conservatism. The results may be summarized as follows:*

Status consciousness—The best prediction for both samples is an intermediate degree of status consciousness.

Attitudes toward authority—All three social classes of the American sample expressed the greatest degree of belief in obedience to constituted authority, with the English sample expressing an intermediate degree of belief.

Political attitudes—The three American social classes expressed the greatest degree of conservatism, while the English classes expressed an intermediate degree of conservatism.

Attitudes toward mobility—The best prediction for both samples is an intermediate degree of consciousness of factors interfering with mobility.

Tolerance for deviant behavior—The best prediction for both samples is the least degree of tolerance for deviant behavior.

Attitudes toward personal habits and manners—The best prediction for the English sample and for the upper and middle classes of the American sample is an intermediate degree of emphasis on personal habits and manners. For the American lower class the greatest degree and intermediate degree are, equally, the best predictions.

Attitudes toward property—The best prediction for both samples is an intermediate degree of seriousness attributed to minor infringements of property rights.

Coefficients of relative predictability for the English and

---

* Since each sample was purposive, not random, and regional, not national, the results can more readily be generalized to the regions from which the samples were taken—the greater London area and urban Washington State—rather than to England and the United States. The extremely high-status segment of the upper social class is not adequately represented in either sample since it was taken from public as opposed to privately supported schools. This discrepancy is more significant in reference to the English sample than it is for the United States.

American samples can be compared in order to determine the relative accuracy of predictions based on social class in the two samples. In twenty-two of the thirty-one questions considered, the C coefficient is zero for both samples. Of the nine remaining questions, the C coefficient is higher for the American sample in four cases and for the English sample in five cases. A positive C coefficient was recorded for at least one question out of six of the seven attitude areas for the English sample, whereas no positive C coefficients were recorded for any question in three of the seven areas of attitudes for the American sample. These results may be summarized as follows: (1) The reduction of errors of prediction, taking social class into account as compared to using the marginal distribution of attitudes, is either zero or close to zero for both samples; (2) where differences did occur, the coefficients were slightly higher for the English sample, with four exceptions.

The calculation of the C' coefficients has as a condition for prediction the following *a priori* rules for the seven attitude areas:

Status consciousness—Upper class most conscious of social distance between the social classes, lower class least conscious.

Attitudes toward authority—Upper class most strongly believes in individual rights to independent thought and action under various types of authority; lower class most firmly believes in obedience to constituted authority.

Political attitudes—Upper class most conservative, lower class most radical.

Attitudes toward mobility—Upper class least conscious of the presence of factors interfering with mobility, lower class most conscious.

Tolerance for deviant behavior—Upper class most tolerant of deviant behavior, middle class least tolerant.

Attitudes toward personal habits and manners—Upper class gives least stress to personal habits and manners, middle class gives most stress.

Attitudes toward property—Upper class considers minor infringements of property rights least serious, lower class considers them most serious.

As with C coefficients, C' coefficients for the two samples can be compared in order to determine the relative accuracy of predictions based on social class in the two samples.

The following is a listing of the seven attitude areas, with the number of questions in each area for which the C' coefficients are higher for the English sample: Status consciousness, three out of five; attitudes toward authority, four out of five; political attitudes, three out of five; attitudes toward mobility, two out of three; tolerance for deviant behavior, three out of five; attitudes toward personal habits and manners, two out of five; and attitudes toward property, one out of three. In five out of the seven attitude areas, the C' coefficients of the English sample were higher than those of the American sample for a majority of the questions. However, the total number of positive C' coefficients for the seven attitude areas is the same for each sample, namely fifteen.

Certain conclusions, within the limitations of the study, are suggested below. Points one and two are made with reference to the first objective of this study: to determine the rules for predicting the attitudes of adolescent boys in the English and the United States samples from their social class. Points three and four are relevant to the second objective: to determine the accuracy of prediction obtained when these rules are used.

1. In the areas of status consciousness, attitudes toward mobility, tolerance for deviant behavior, attitudes toward personal habits and manners, and attitudes toward property, the best rules for prediction for the classes in the English sample were the same as for the American sample.

2. In the areas of attitudes toward authority and political attitudes, differences between the samples were found for all classes in the direction of a greater degree of conservatism, with respect to conformity to established institutional patterns on the part of the American sample.

3. Using the principle of maximum probability the reduction of errors of prediction, taking social class into account as compared with using the marginal distribution of attitudes, is either zero or close to zero for both samples. Where differences oc-

curred, the coefficients were slightly higher for the English sample, with four exceptions.

4. Using another prediction technique, involving the calculation of C' coefficients, it was possible to differentiate between the effectiveness of social class as a predictor of the various attitude areas in each of the samples. Social class tends to be a better predictor, using the *a priori* rules for prediction, for the English sample than for the American sample in the following areas of attitudes: status consciousness, political attitudes, attitudes toward mobility, tolerance for deviant behavior, and attitudes toward authority. With respect to attitudes toward personal habits and manners and toward property, social class tends to be a better predictor for the American sample.

chapter seventeen

ANXIETY AMONG ENGLISH AND
AMERICAN BOYS*

Anxiety is frequently a basic factor in adjustment to problem situations. If the anxiety evidenced is not disproportionate to the objective situation and if adjustment can be achieved by rational behavior, the anxiety factor is termed normal, or adaptive. On the other hand, if the anxiety exhibited is disproportionate to the objective situation and adjustive behavior involves repression and the development of neurotic symptoms, the anxiety factor is thought of as abnormal, or "neurotic anxiety."[19] Thus the individual's definition of the situation determines the kind of anxiety generated.

It seems doubtful that this distinction between normal and abnormal anxiety should be utilized in reference to nationality groups or social classes. However, the comparative frequency of expression of generic anxiety by individuals composing a group or class can be ascertained and inferences may be drawn about existing differences in their definitions of objective situations. The term anxiety as used in this study does not imply pathology (although neurotic anxiety may have been present in some individuals). Rather, it refers to an emotional expression of uncertainty, unusual concern, or apprehension. In this generic sense, it is assumed that the response "worried me a lot" to a check-list item indicates the presence of some degree of anxiety in the respondent.

The respondents were samples of English and American

* From *American Sociological Review*, Vol. XXI, No. 2, 1956, revised and enlarged.

thirteen- and fourteen-year-old boys, thus permitting comparisons to be made by nationality groups as well as by social class. The English sample consisted of six hundred boys from selected grammar and secondary modern schools in greater London. The United States sample was taken from the same age-group in high schools in Seattle and Spokane, Washington, and numbered 744. In selecting the samples in both countries, an attempt was made to approximate representativeness in terms of the occupations of the boys' fathers. After study of the ecology of the cities and with a general knowledge of the socio-economic characteristics of various school populations in each city, a selection of schools was made. All thirteen- and fourteen-year-old boys in attendance when the questionnaire was administered constituted the samples.* Each nationality group was divided into three social-class groups upon the basis of the prestige of the occupations of the boys' fathers.† The number in each social-class group was as follows: English I, (upper) 89; English II, 349; English III, 162; U.S. I, 242; U.S. II, 320; U.S. III, 182.

Both samples responded to the same worries check list. The check list provided for three possible responses: "worries me a lot," "worries me a little," and "does not worry me." In this analysis the responses were dichotomized by combining the responses in the second and third categories. Items were selected from the check list and regrouped with reference to certain social situations: the family and sibling relations; situations involving self-confidence; concern for material symbols of social status; school situations; and relations with girls. The discussion of these areas is in terms of percentage distribution of responses

---

* Chi square analysis of the Seattle-Spokane sample based on census occupational data shows that, for a sample of this size, departures from theoretical expectations as large as or larger than those found could occur by chance about 4 per cent of the time under the assumption of random selection. Comparable census data was not available to permit a similar analysis of the London sample.

† A correlation of .89 was found between the prestige ranking represented by the Edwards Census Classification and those of the English Standard Classification. This permitted equating certain occupational categories of the two classifications and thus coding both samples by a slightly modified Edwards Classification.

TABLE 9—*Percentage Distribution of Anxiety Responses by Social Class*

Statement Which "Worries Me a Lot"	Social Class I		Social Class II		Social Class III	
	U.S. N = 242	England N = 89	U.S. N = 320	England N = 349	U.S. N = 182	England N = 162
A* Relative to parents & siblings:						
Mother does not treat me right	31.0	25.8	29.1	30.1	22.0	35.8
Father does not treat me right	24.8	23.6	19.1	26.4	17.6	29.0
Parents expect too much of me	19.0	28.1	20.3	24.4	15.9	26.5
Parents do not understand me	28.5	29.3	27.8	40.1	21.4	38.3
Parents do not seem to care enough for me	28.9	38.2	23.4	37.3	27.5	40.1
Do not know how to show parents how much I care for them	25.2	48.3	29.1	55.3	26.4	56.2
Parents want me to be a different kind of boy	21.1	28.1	19.7	26.9	22.0	29.6
My brothers and sisters seem to do things better than I can	7.4	6.7	6.6	9.7	7.1	15.4
Parents like my brothers and sisters better than me	14.9	19.1	12.8	12.3	13.2	17.3
Mean	22.3	28.6	20.9	29.2	19.2	32.0

B* Relative to self-adequacy:						
Lack self-confidence	35.1	40.5	31.9	43.0	27.5	49.4
Feel inferior	23.6	15.7	15.6	20.1	9.9	22.2
Have to take second place to other boys	16.1	18.0	10.3	19.5	14.8	19.1
Feel like an outsider	22.3	32.6	18.8	31.8	18.7	25.3
Not popular	28.5	36.0	25.6	33.8	17.0	34.0
Tire easily	21.9	24.7	14.1	29.5	17.0	33.3
Mean	24.6	27.9	19.4	29.6	17.5	30.6
C* Relative to material symbols of status:						
Want to live in a nicer house	3.3	5.6	3.1	13.8	6.0	17.3
Too few nice clothes	8.7	19.1	8.1	27.5	11.5	29.0
Have less money than others	7.0	14.6	3.8	14.3	6.6	27.2
Not enough money for pleasure	10.3	15.7	12.8	17.8	10.1	25.9
Mean	7.3	13.8	7.0	18.4	8.6	24.9
D* Relative to girls:						
Think too much about girls	8.3	15.7	7.2	14.0	6.6	13.0
Want to have a girl friend	14.9	21.3	16.3	20.1	13.7	21.0
Do not mix well with girls	21.1	18.0	21.6	26.1	23.6	24.1
Girls make fun of me	26.9	22.5	24.7	17.2	20.3	13.6
Mean	17.8	19.4	17.5	19.4	16.1	17.9

* The weighted national means for each area are: (A) U.S., 20.9; England, 29.9; (B) U.S., 20.6; England, 29.6; (C) U.S., 7.5; England, 19.5; (D) U.S., 17.3; England, 19.0. United States (N = 744); England (N = 600).

by nationality group and social class. The mean of responses by class and nationality has also been computed.

It is felt that before summarizing the findings and pointing to some implications, the major limitations of the study should be stated: (1) the samples probably do not meet the assumptions of tests of significance. Thus statistical analysis has been limited to a consideration of percentage distributions by class and nationality and to computing means of these percentages. (2) Although both samples responded to the same items composing a "worries check list," different cultural definitions may have been brought to bear on the items. (3) Although the social-class groups in each country were composed of boys whose fathers have similar occupational prestige in both countries, social class is a part of the national culture and may be defined in somewhat different ways in each society. Thus the variables of nationality and social class cannot be completely separated. With these limitations in mind and being cognizant of the exploratory nature of the study, the findings may be summarized as follows.

Table 9 presents the basic data in number and per cent by nationality and social class. There is considerable consistency of response by nationality group. In each area, nationality differences are greater than class differences. The English boys evidence what appears to be significantly more concern than do the American boys in relation to their parents and siblings, self-adequacy, and symbols of status. The nationality differences are slight, however, in feelings about girls—the English boys showing more concern, particularly in the more covert behavior.

When compared by social class, the greatest differences are found between English III and U.S. III (the two working classes) except for the statements concerning girls, in which instance the differences are slight. Social class differences within the nationality groups are consistently small. Distinguishable trends may be noted, however, in relation to each category. English III appears to be the most concerned about relations with parents and siblings and English II the least, whereas U.S. I and II are somewhat more disturbed than is U.S. III about these relationships. A similar trend is seen in relation to self-adequacy, but the differences may be too small to be meaningful. In the area concerned with status symbols, English III evidences the most concern and English I the least; differences between the U.S. social classes are small. Class differences in relation to girls do not appear to be significant in either nationality group.

It should be emphasized that anxiety, as defined here, does not imply pathology, but rather may be a factor in adjustment to social reality.*

---

* It should be noted that at the time this study was made (1950–51 in England and 1952–54 in the U.S.) England was still suffering from World War II. It was a period of shortages; food was rationed, rents were controlled, and housing was in short supply. Classrooms were crowded as a result of the lack of school buildings. At the same time, it was a period of political change and gradual economic recovery. The influence of the general "abnormal" cultural situation upon the responses of the English boys is unknown. The situation in the United States was certainly much different.

chapter eighteen

ATTITUDES TOWARD SOCIAL MOBILITY AS REVEALED BY NEGRO AND WHITE BOYS IN THE UNITED STATES*

Equal opportunity for upward mobility is a basic myth in our society. It is enshrined in the American Creed and is thought to be a widespread motivating force in the formation of the aspirations of young Americans. There is much striving toward improving one's economic and social status. Some students have considered the high value put upon material success to be the very basis of American national character.

The purpose of this study is to analyze comparative data on concepts of the class structure and attitudes toward mobility held by Negro and white boys from two geocultural areas—the Pacific Northwest and the Deep South. Attitudes of Negro boys from the Deep South are compared with those of white boys from the Pacific Northwest to determine what bearing the findings might have upon the concept of national character.

There is a tendency in national character studies to take an essentially unimodal view of a national culture. A few basic cultural themes which have been identified and analyzed are thought to characterize the entire society. Such uniformities in culture are then related to "basic personality structure." This approach largely ignores the possibility of a multi-modal national culture.[20] Geocultural areas, social classes, diverse religious

---

* From *The Pacific Sociological Review*, I, 2, 1958, published jointly with Edgar C. Epps.

groups and nationality and racial minorities may represent
cultural subgroups and behavioral modalities which would place
considerable doubt upon the concept of national character in
any form other than an unverified theoretical construct.

With reference to the Negro minority, Hylan Lewis says,
"Negro society in the United States is shaped and guided to a
significant extent by an evolving national subculture, which,
although a variant of the national culture, exhibits growth,
patterning, and a gross national 'character' all its own."[21]

Thus, by comparing attitudes toward mobility as expressed
by Negro and white boys in different geographical areas of the
United States we may, in a limited way, examine the plausibility
of the assumption of a high degree of cultural homogeneity
and the related concept of national character.

The data for this study were obtained by means of a questionnaire which was administered to 744 white* thirteen- and
fourteen-year-old school boys from Seattle and Spokane, Washington, and from 498 Negro boys of the same age from the
segregated schools of several cities in the Deep South.† Each
sample was broken down into social-class groups: upper (professional and managerial); middle (largely clerical, sales, super-

---

* The Seattle-Spokane sample included small numbers of Negro and
Mongoloid boys.

† Originally, requests to administer the questionnaire were made to the
administrators of both Negro and white schools in the Deep South. Because only one administrator of the white schools was willing to administer
the hour-long questionnaire, and all of the Negro schools contacted were
willing to cooperate, we acquired, in the end, an all-Negro sample.
The schools cooperating in Seattle and Spokane were selected after a
careful study of the ecology of the cities. Comparison of the distribution of
occupations of the boys' fathers with the U.S. Census occupational data
for the two cities revealed that the sample closely approached representativeness. The cooperating schools in the South were selected through persons known to the writers. How closely they approach a representative sample is not known. The schools were located in large cities in Alabama and
Florida. Although statistical tests of significance have been used with the
data experimentally, they are not included in this paper because of the
probability that the samples do not meet the assumptions of such tests. The
terms "Deep South sample" and "Seattle-Spokane sample" are used for
convenience. Generalizing to either racial or regional population is hazardous.

visory, and artisans); and working (semi-skilled, unskilled, and service workers). This breakdown was based upon a modified Alba Edwards classification. It was found for purposes of this analysis, that it was advantageous to combine the upper and middle groups in both samples, which resulted in a non-manual–manual breakdown, considering clerical workers as non-manual. The size of each social-class group was as follows: Seattle-Spokane (white), Class I (non-manual), 562; Class II (manual), 182; Deep South (Negro), Class I, 100; Class II, 308.

The analysis which follows is limited to a consideration of the questions and responses dealing with social mobility, social class, and related subjects. This is the area in which the greatest disparity between the two groups was observed. The responses to these questions brought out certain inconsistencies in the attitudes of both groups by revealing wide acceptance of their present position in society and at the same time indicating general acceptance of the desirability of upward mobility. This may represent the disparity between the "ideal culture" and the "real culture." In other words, there is a conflict between what is and what ought to be. This conflict is most evident in the responses of the Deep South sample.

Table 10 presents the affirmative responses to our inquiries. The first statement, "We are all born to our various social positions and it would not do to change them," was more widely accepted by the Deep South group than it was by the boys from Seattle-Spokane. Thirty-one per cent of Class I and 40 per cent of Class II among the Deep South boys accepted this statement. The idea was not as widely accepted among the Seattle-Spokane group where the corresponding percentages were 15.1 and 24.2. Thus, social-class differences are present in that Class II in both groups is more likely to accept the statement as true. However, the class difference is not as great as the difference between the regional groups. It seems likely that this statement was interpreted by many of the Negro respondents in racial terms. In recognition of the social reality, a large percentage of the Deep South sample may have accepted the severe limitations placed upon upward mobility in the South.

The statement that "It is wrong for a person to be dissatisfied

TABLE 10—*Percentage Distribution of Affirmative Responses**

Item	Question	Seattle-Spokane (White)		Deep South (Negro)	
		Class I	Class II	Class I	Class II
1.	We are all born to our various social positions and it would not do to change them	15.1	24.2	31.0	40.0
2.	It is wrong for a person to be dissatisfied with his position in life	26.0	34.1	50.0	48.4
3.	The way to be happy in life is to be satisfied with whatever you have	60.4	64.9	80.1	78.6
4.	The select few must be trained to lead the common herd of people	25.1	24.7	43.0	52.6
5.	Some classes of people are not as good as other classes	29.0	29.7	58.0	62.3
6.	It is best not to marry someone who comes from a different kind of home from one's own	8.7	4.9	20.0	64.0
7.	Most boys should try to get a better job than their fathers have	40.0	43.0	60.0	59.1
8.	If a person doesn't do better than his father did, he is no good	3.9	7.0	12.0	21.1
9.	It is only right that the strong should rule the weak	9.6	9.2	11.0	14.9
10.	It is wrong that some classes of people have much more money than others	21.7	24.7	79.0	20.5
11.	Everybody should have the same amount of money	11.7	18.7	7.0	11.7
12.	Education is not good for some people because it only makes them dissatisfied with everything	11.6	14.8	19.0	23.1
13.	Some boys have a better chance in life than others	70.1	69.8	74.0	80.2
14.	The world is full of possibilities open to everyone	82.7	77.6	81.0	74.7

* Other response categories were "disagree," "uncertain," and "no response." Seattle-Spokane (White) Class I, N = 262, Class II, N = 182; Deep South (Negro) Class I, N = 100, Class II, N = 308.

with his position in life" was also more widely accepted by the
Deep South group than by the Seattle-Spokane group. Half of
the boys in the Deep South sample agreed to this statement,
while only a quarter of the Seattle-Spokane group accepted it.
Here again, the class differences are not as great as are the
differences between the two samples. It is reasonable to believe
that the same "racial" factor was operating in this case. If the
statement was interpreted in racial terms, it may have seemed
to read: "It is wrong to be dissatisfied because you happen to
be a Negro."

The same idea, stated positively, "The way to be happy in
life is to be satisfied with whatever you have," received even
more agreement from both regional groups. Approximately 80
per cent of the Deep South sample and 62 per cent of the
Seattle-Spokane sample agreed with this statement.

Responses to the statement that "The select few must be
trained to lead the common herd of people" revealed similar
differences between the two samples. Class differences are
slight for both populations, but the per cent of the Deep South
sample agreeing with the statement is approximately twice that
of the Seattle-Spokane sample. A "racial" interpretation among
the Negro boys in terms of social reality where most positions
of leadership are filled by white men may have influenced these
responses. Also, some of these boys' responses may have been
influenced by having heard from their teachers, parents, or
community leaders the proposition put forth by Dr. W. E. B.
Du Bois, that the "talented tenth" must lead the Negroes out of
second-class citizenship.

Another statement which elicited considerably more acceptance from the Deep South group than from the Seattle-Spokane
group was: "Some classes of people are not as good as other
classes." Approximately 60 per cent of the Deep South sample
agreed with this statement as compared to 29 per cent of the
Seattle-Spokane sample. Due to the wording of the question,
responses in each group were apt to be in moral terms. However,
the responses of the Deep South group may have been influenced
by existing differential achievement and status levels of whites
and Negroes.

The responses of the two groups to the statement that "It is best not to marry someone who comes from a different kind of home from one's own," would indicate that class lines are drawn somewhat more tightly among the Deep South sample than in the Seattle-Spokane sample. Twenty per cent of Deep South Class I and 64 per cent of Deep South Class II accepted this statement. Only 9 per cent of Seattle-Spokane Class I and 5 per cent of Seattle-Spokane Class II found this statement acceptable. It appears likely that some of the Negro boys were thinking in terms of racial intermarriage. This is a connotation which the white group would not have placed upon the question.

Items 7 and 8 in Table 10 deal more directly with upward mobility. The responses to item 7, "Most boys should try to get a better job than their fathers have," indicate that there is somewhat more acceptance of the statement among the Deep South sample than among the Seattle-Spokane sample. There is widespread aspiration for improving one's status in both groups. The responses of the Deep South group tended to contradict more strongly their previous responses than is true of the Seattle-Spokane sample. For instance, 50 per cent of the Deep South had already said that it is wrong to be dissatisfied with one's position in life while 60 per cent now hold that boys should try to get better jobs than their fathers have.

It is likely that both samples interpreted the statement literally to mean they should try to get better jobs. If so, this may represent aspirations for mobility within the widely accepted class structure and not necessarily mean that they should try to change their social class status. Responses to the second statement, "If a person doesn't do better than his father did, he is no good," showed that the large majority of each sample rejected the idea.

The remaining statements did not reveal significant differences in responses of either the regional groups or social classes. These statements, items 9-14 in Table 10, are probably more closely related, positively or negatively, to the widely accepted ideal culture of the societies.

Table 11 presents the data for two questions having to do with chances for upward mobility. Responses to the first question,

Table 11—Percentage Distribution of Responses Concerning Comparative Chances for Upward Mobility by Region and Class

| Question | Seattle-Spokane (White) | | | | | | | | Deep South (Negro) | | | | | | | |
| | Class I N = 562 | | | | Class II N = 182 | | | | Class I N = 100 | | | | Class II N = 308 | | | |
	As Good A Chance	A Better Chance	A Poorer Chance	No Response	As Good A Chance	A Better Chance	A Poorer Chance	No Response	As Good A Chance	A Better Chance	A Poorer Chance	No Response	As Good A Chance	A Better Chance	A Poorer Chance	No Response
Do you think you have as good a chance as other boys of moving up in the world?	87.0	10.7	1.4	0.9	92.3	5.5	1.6	0.5	75.0	19.0	3.0	3.0	71.1	24.3	2.3	2.3
Do you think you have as good a chance as your father had of moving up in the world?	40.7	54.8	3.6	0.9	35.7	60.4	3.3	0.5	21.0	75.0	1.0	3.0	25.3	70.5	1.0	3.2

"Do you think that you have as good a chance as other boys of moving up in the world?," reveal that a larger proportion (19.0 per cent) of the Deep South sample considered that they had a "better chance" of moving up in the world than was true of the Seattle-Spokane sample (10.7 per cent).

The difference is even more marked for the second question: "Do you think that you have as good a chance as your father had of moving up in the world?" Here 75.0 per cent of the Deep South sample held they had a "better chance" as compared to 54.8 per cent for the Seattle-Spokane group.

It may be that the Deep South sample read, in the first question, "other Negro boys" for "other boys." It would seem reasonable to assume that some of the respondents did so interpret the question. These boys had succeeded in staying in school for one reason or other and all of them were attending city schools which were superior to most of the schools for Negroes in the South.

A similar question arose in regard to the phrase "moving up in the world"—what world? In answer to this question, many of the Negro boys might have been thinking of the "colored world," that is, in terms of the existing class structure among the Negro population. Or, on the other hand, their responses could indicate a cognizance of expanding opportunities for Negroes in our society.

The second question refers specifically to "your father" and does not raise the question of race. However, the same ambiguity exists in reference to "what world." Regardless of the referent, a larger percentage of the Deep South sample than of the Seattle-Spokane group was convinced that they have a better chance than their fathers had.

The general optimism and evidence of high aspiration level revealed in the responses of the Deep South sample to these last two questions makes even more clear the basic confusion and existing conflict in the thinking of this group about the social structure and mobility. This situation is not peculiar to the Deep South sample alone but is much more in evidence there. It appears that the "racial factor" accounts, at least in part, for this difference and possibly for most of the significant differences between the two samples.

Certain recurrent difficulties in interpreting responses to the questionnaire are recognized. It is impossible to know with certainty whether or not the respondent's reference group was racial, regional, or stratificational. It may be safely assumed that in the Seattle-Spokane group a racial frame of reference was most unlikely. However, among the Negro boys of the Deep South sample, social position may be conceived of largely in racial terms. By racial terms is meant existing social relationships between the races. Also, when responses appear to be in social class terms we cannot be certain which of three stratification systems (Negro, white, or community) serves as the reference group.* For the purposes of this study, however, the focal point is the total subcultural influence rather than specific reference groups.

Being mindful of the limitations of the study, it would appear that the attitudinal differences relative to social mobility between the two samples are substantial and arise primarily from subcultural variability. The Deep South has its own characteristic system of social stratification that has developed from an historical-cultural background differing from that of other regions in the United States. This social structure is complicated by racial factors which differ in degree, if not in kind, from those found in other regions. We were unable to identify the specific cultural complexes responsible for the differences in attitudinal responses which were exhibited between the two groups. We do not know whether or not the responses of our Negro boys are similar to responses which would be elicited from white boys in the Deep South. As desirable as it admittedly would be to have the kinds of data necessary to answer these questions, such data are not vital to the purpose of the study, which was to demonstrate differences in attitudes toward

---

* In dealing with this problem, the writers were greatly assisted by the interpretations of Mr. James W. Kelsaw and Mr. James E. Blackwell. Their insights, as well as those of Mr. Epps, are based upon their present ability as sociologists to analyze their own previous experiences in segregated groups in the Deep South.

social mobility between two large groups of boys of the same nationality and age group but of different race and region of residence. Such differences have been shown to exist and therefore, in the study of national character, the assumption of a high degree of homogeneity of culture that tends to ignore regional and "racial" differences in relation to basic personality would seem to be inaccurate and unjustified.

NOTES

Notes to Introduction and Part I

1. "Manifesto of the Communist Party," in *Karl Marx and Frederick Engels, Selected Works* (Moscow: Foreign Languages Publishing House, 1950), I, 42. (Italics mine.)

2. See Ralph Linton, "Problems of Status Personality," in *Culture and Personality*, eds. S. Sargent and M. Smith (New York: Viking Fund, 1949), p. 167.

3. See A. R. Lindesmith and A. L. Strauss, "A Critique of Culture-Personality Writings," *American Sociological Review*, XV (1950), 587-600.

4. Max Lerner, "The Idea of American Civilization," *Journal of Social Issues*, Vol. VII, No. 4 (1951), p. 31.

5. T. B. Bottomore and Maximilien Rubel (eds.), *Karl Marx, Selected Writings in Sociology and Social Philosophy* (London: Watts and Co., 1956), p. 23.

6. Rolf Dahrendorf, *Class and Class Conflict in Industrial Society* (Stanford: Stanford University Press, 1959), pp. 9-18.

7. In addition to Dahrendorf's chapter, "Marx's Model," *Ibid.*, see Reinhard Bendix and Seymour Lipset, "Marx's Theory of Social Class," in Reinhard Bendix and Seymour Lipset (eds.), *Class, Status and Power* (Glencoe: The Free Press, 1953), and Bottomore and Rubel, *op. cit.*; C. Wright Mills, *The Marxists*, Dell, New York.

8. Bottomore and Rubel, *Ibid.*, p. 178.

9. *Marx and Engels Selected Works*, I, *op. cit.*, p. 33.

10. *Ibid.*

11. *Ibid.*, p. 41.

12. *Ibid.*, pp. 443-44.

13. For American studies using a Marxian frame of reference to some extent, see Lewis Corey, *The Crisis of the Middle Class* (New York: Covici-Friede, 1935); Robert S. Lynd and Helen M. Lynd, *Middletown* (New York: Harcourt, Brace, 1929); Robert S. Lynd and Helen M. Lynd, *Middletown in Transition* (New York: Harcourt, Brace, 1937); Richard Centers, *The Psychology of Social Classes* (Princeton: Princeton University Press, 1949); and Oliver Cromwell Cox, *Class, Caste and Race* (New York: Doubleday, 1948).

14. Reinhard Bendix, *Max Weber, An Intellectual Portrait* (Garden City: Doubleday and Co., 1960), p. 266. This section

draws heavily upon Bendix's chapter, "Max Weber's Image of Society."

15. *Ibid.*, p. 268.

16. Max Weber, *The Protestant Ethic and the Spirit of Capitalism* (London: George Allen and Unwin, 1930).

17. Bendix and Lipset, *op. cit.*, pp. 267-68.

18. *Ibid.*, p. 105. Weber's original statement was so stilted and poorly written that his interpreters have had the responsibility for making it intelligible. This statement is a rearrangement by Bendix of Gerth and Mills's formulation. See H. H. Gerth and C. Wright Mills, *From Max Weber* (London: Kegan Paul, Trench, Trubner, and Co., Ltd., 1947), pp. 181-82.

19. Bendix, *op. cit.*, p. 105.

20. *Ibid.*, pp. 105-6—a reformulation from Gerth and Mills, *op. cit.*, pp. 186-87, 187-88, and 190-91.

21. *Ibid.*, p. 183.

22. *Ibid.*, pp. 183, 192.

23. *Ibid.*, pp. 184-85.

24. *Ibid.*, p. 193.

25. *Ibid.*, p. 194.

26. *Ibid.*

27. *Ibid.*, pp. 194, 195.

28. For American works using a Weberian frame of reference to some extent, see Kurt B. Mayer, *Class and Society* (Garden City: Doubleday and Co., 1955); Joseph Kahl, *The American Class Structure* (New York: Rinehart and Co., Inc., 1953); and Leonard Reissman, *Class in American Society* (Glencoe: Free Press, 1959), p. xi.

29. Talcott Parsons, "A Revised Analytical Approach to the Theory of Social Stratification," in Bendix and Lipset, *Class, Status and Power, op. cit.*, p. 93.

30. The most pertinent papers are: Kingsley Davis, "A Conceptual Analysis of Stratification," *ASR*, 7 (June, 1942), pp. 309-21; Kingsley Davis and Wilbert E. Moore, "Some Principles of Stratification," *ASR*, X (April, 1945), pp. 242-49; Melvin Tumin, "Some Principles of Stratification: A Critical Analysis," *ASR*, XVIII (Aug., 1953), pp. 387-94; Davis and Moore, "Reply and Comment," *Ibid.*, pp. 394-97; Walter Buckley, "Social Stratification and Functional Theory of Social Differentiation," *ASR*, XXIII (Aug., 1958), pp. 369-75; Kingsley Davis, Marion J. Levy, Jr., and Walter Buckley, "Stratification and Functionalism: An Exchange," *ASR*, XXIV (Feb., 1959), pp. 82-86; Kingsley Davis, "The Myth of Functional Analysis," *ASR*, XXIV (Dec., 1959), pp. 757-72; and Dennis H. Wrong, "The Functional Theory of Stratification: Some Neglected Considerations," *ASR*, XXIV (Dec., 1959), pp. 772-82. Also see: "Introduction," in Bendix and Lipset, *Class, Status and Power, op. cit.*, pp. 7-16.

31. Davis and Moore, "Some Principles of Stratification," *op. cit.*
32. *Ibid.*, p. 242.
33. *Ibid.*, p. 243.
34. *Ibid.*
35. *Ibid.*, p. 244.
36. Tumin, *op. cit.*
37. *Ibid.*, p. 389.
38. *Ibid.*
39. *Ibid.*, p. 391.
40. *Ibid.*, pp. 392-93.
41. *Ibid.*, p. 393. See discussion on nationality.
42. Buckley, "Social Stratification and Functional Theory," *op. cit.*
43. *Ibid.*, p. 370.
44. *Ibid.*, p. 372.
45. *Ibid.*, p. 373.
46. For Davis and Moore's "rebuttals," see Davis and Moore, "Reply and Comment," *op. cit.*, and Davis, Levy and Buckley, "Stratification and Functionalism: An Exchange," *op. cit.*
47. Bendix and Lipset, *Class, Status and Power, op. cit.*, p. 13.
48. Buckley, "Social Stratification and Functional Theory," *op. cit.*, n. 29, p. 374.
49. Bendix and Lipset, *op. cit.*, p. 13.
50. Seymour M. Lipset and Neil J. Smelser, *Sociology, The Progress of a Decade,* (Englewood Cliffs, New Jersey: Prentice Hall, 1961), p. 5.
51. *Ibid.*, p. 7.
52. For American works in addition to the Warner School, utilizing to some extent a functionalist frame of reference, see Bernard Barber, *Social Stratification* (New York: Harcourt, Brace and Co., 1957), and John F. Cuber and William F. Kenkel, *Social Stratification in the United States* (New York: Appleton-Century-Crofts, 1954).
53. W. Lloyd Warner and Paul S. Lunt, *The Social Life of a Modern Community* (New Haven: Yale University Press, 1941).
54. *Ibid.*, p. 3.
55. *Ibid.*, as seen in Chapter II, pp. 9-37.
56. *Ibid.*, p. 81.
57. *Ibid.*, p. 82.
58. W. Lloyd Warner, Marchia Meeker and Kenneth Eells, *Social Class in America* (Chicago: Science Research Associates, 1949). Until this book was published, no one knew in any detail what Warner's method really was.
59. W. Lloyd Warner, *Democracy in Jonesville* (New York: Harper and Brothers, 1949).
60. *Ibid.*, pp. xiii-xiv.

61. *Ibid.*, pp. xiv-xv.

62. C. Wright Mills's review of *The Social Life of a Modern Community*, *ASR*, VII (April, 1942), pp. 263-71; Harold W. Pfautz and Otis Dudley Duncan, "A Critical Evaluation of Warner's work in Community Stratification," *ASR*, XV (April, 1950), pp. 205-15; S. M. Lipset and R. Bendix, "Social Status and Social Structure," Part I, *British Journal of Sociology*, II (June, 1951), pp. 150-68 and Part II, *British Journal of Sociology*, II (Sept., 1951), pp. 230-54; Joel B. Montague, Jr., "Class or Status Society," *Sociology and Social Research*, XL (May-June, 1956), pp. 333-38.

63. Lipset and Bendix, "Social Status and Social Structure," Part I, *op. cit.*, p. 162.

64. Mills's review of *The Social Life of a Modern Community*, *op. cit.*, p. 263.

65. Lipset and Bendix, "Social Status and Social Structure," Part II, *op. cit.*, p. 246.

66. *Ibid.*, p. 242.

67. Mills's review, *op. cit.*

68. *Ibid.*, p. 266.

69. Lipset and Bendix, "Social Status and Social Structure," Part I, *op. cit.*, p. 150.

70. Karl W. Deutsch, *Nationalism and Social Communication* (New York: The Technology Press of the Mass. Institute of Technology and John Wiley and Sons, Inc., 1953), pp. 70-74.

71. *Ibid.*, p. 71. See Max Huber, "Swiss Nationality," in *Modern Political Doctrines*, ed. by Sir Alfred Zimmern (London: Oxford University Press, 1939), pp. 216-17.

72. Florian Znaniecki, *Modern Nationalities* (Urbana: University of Illinois Press, 1952).

73. Frederick Hertz, *Nationality in History and Politics* (New York: Oxford Univeristy Press, 1944), p. 87.

74. Walter Sulzbach, *National Consciousness* (Washington, D.C.: American Council on Public Affairs, 1943), pp. 8-9.

75. J. Novicow, *Conscience et Volonté Sociales* (Paris: 1897), as quoted by Walter Sulzbach, *Ibid.*, pp. 12-13.

76. *Ibid.*, p. 10.

77. *Ibid.*, p. 11.

78. *Ibid.*, p. 14.

79. Frederick Hertz, *op. cit.*, pp. 6-7.

80. *Ibid.*, p. 235.

81. J. Fievée, *Lettres sur l'Angleterre et Réflexions sur la Philosophie du XVIII Siècle*, 1802, as quoted by Hertz, *op. cit.*, p. 235.

82. E. H. Carr, *Nationalism and After* (London: MacMillan Co., Ltd., 1945), p. 10.

83. *Ibid.*, pp. 18-19.

84. *Ibid.*, p. 19.

85. Deutsch, *op. cit.*, p. 70.

86. Carr, *op. cit.*, p. 38.

87. *Ibid.*, p. 39.

88. Ralph Linton, *The Cultural Background of Personality* (New York: D. Appleton Century Co., 1945), pp. 128-29.

89. Ralph Linton, "The Concept of National Character," in Alfred H. Stanton and Stewart E. Perry (eds.), *Personality and Political Crisis* (Glencoe: Free Press, 1951), p. 140.

90. Alex Inkeles and Daniel J. Levinson, "National Character: The Study of Modal Personality and Socio-cultural Systems," in G. Lindzey (ed.), *Handbook of Social Psychology* (Cambridge: Addison-Wesley Publishing Co., 1954), p. 983.

91. G. Gorer, "The Concept of National Character," *Science News*, XVIII (Nov., 1950), p. 117.

92. *Ibid.*, p. 112.

93. Margaret Mead, "National Character," in A. L. Kroeber (ed.), *Anthropology Today* (Chicago: The University of Chicago Press, 1953), p. 642.

94. Gorer, *op. cit.*, pp. 106-9.

95. Mead in Kroeber, *op. cit.*, p. 442.

96. Ralph Linton in Stanton and Perry, *op. cit.*, p. 134.

97. Abram Kardiner, *The Individual and Society* (New York: Columbia University Press, 1945), pp. 107-22 and Erich Fromm, *Escape from Freedom* (New York: Farrar and Rinehart, 1941).

98. Inkeles and Levinson in Lindzey, *op. cit.*, p. 980.

99. *Ibid.*, p. 982.

100. Gorer, *op. cit.*, pp. 107-8.

101. See Linton in Stanton and Perry, *op. cit.*, pp. 135-37.

102. G. Gorer in Margaret Mead and Rhoda Metraux, *The Study of Culture at a Distance* (Chicago: University of Chicago Press, 1953), p. 67.

103. Mead in Kroeber, *op. cit.*, pp. 646-48.

104. *Ibid.*, p. 648. (Italics Mead's.)

105. *Ibid.*

106. Linton in Stanton and Perry, *op. cit.*, p. 135.

107. H. V. Dicks, "Personality Traits and National Socialist Ideology," *Human Relations*, 1950, III, pp. 111-54, and his "Observations on Contemporary Russian Behavior," 1952, pp. 111-75.

108. See G. Bateson and M. Mead, *Balinese Character: A Photographic Analysis* (New York: Academy of Science, 1942); G. Gorer, "Themes in Japanese Culture," *Transactions of the New York Academy of Science*, 1943, Series II, Vol. 5, pp. 106-24; and M. E. Opler, "Themes as Dynamic Forces in Culture," *ASR*, 1945, LI, pp. 198-206.

109. See Bateson and Mead, *op. cit.*; Cora DuBois, *The People of Alor* (Minneapolis: University of Minnesota Press, 1944); E. H. Erickson, *Childhood and Society* (New York: Norton and Co., 1950); G. Gorer and J. Rickman, *The People of Great Russia* (London: Crosset Press, 1949).

110. Inkeles and Levinson, *op. cit.*, pp. 997-98.

Notes to Part II

1. Robert Bierstedt, "An Analysis of Social Power," *ASR,* XV (Dec., 1950), 730-38.

2. See G. D. H. Cole, "The Conception of the Middle Classes," *British Journal of Sociology,* I (Dec., 1950), 275-90.

3. R. H. Gretton, *The English Middle Class* (London: G. Bell and Sons, Ltd., 1919), pp. 1-10.

4. A. M. Carr-Saunders and D. Caradog Jones, *A Survey of the Social Structure of England and Wales,* 2d ed. (Oxford, at the Clarendon Press, 1937), pp. 66 and 67. They say further, "We have employed various methods of classifying the population and no methods as yet used have brought to light the existence of social classes" (p. 66). However, they admit that social classes may exist, and find the working class the easiest to identify.

5. Roy Lewis and Angus Maude, *The English Middle Classes* (London: Phoenix House, 1949), p. 17.

6. *News Chronicle,* London, April 29, 1949.

7. Cole, *op. cit.*, p. 288.

8. Morris Ginsberg, *Sociology* (London: Oxford University Press, 1934), p. 170.

9. "The Middle Class Argument," *Spectator,* June 20, 1949– Feb. 17, 1950; "Twilight of the Middle Classes," *Roundtable* (June, 1947), pp. 219-24; also see Lewis and Maude, *op. cit.*, pp. 273-89.

10. J. L. and Barbara Hammond, *The Town Laborer 1760-1832,* I (Guild Books, London: Longman's Green and Company, Ltd., 1949); G. D. H. Cole and Raymond Postgate, *The Common People,* 4th ed. (London: Methuen and Co., Ltd., 1949), pp. 117-50.

11. G. D. H. Cole, *Short History of the British Working-Class Movement, 1789-1937,* revised (London: Allen and Unwin, 1937); G. D. H. Cole and Raymond Postgate, *op. cit.*; also see Francis Williams, *Fifty Years' March* (London: Oldhams Press, Ltd.).

12. Carr-Saunders and Jones, *op. cit.*, p. 67.

13. R. H. Tawney, *Equality* (London: George Allen and Unwin, Ltd., 1931), p. 80. Professor Tawney, in conversation with the writer, has commented that the *social* unity of this diverse group is

based upon the acceptance of a common ideology, whereas the "upper classes" are unified by a customary way of life.

14. Lewis and Maude, *op. cit.*, p. 17.

15. G. D. H. Cole, "The Conception of the Middle Classes," *loc. cit.*, p. 287.

16. Ginsberg, *op. cit.*, pp. 167-68.

17. Bierstedt, *op. cit.*, p. 737.

18. Tawney, *op. cit.*, p. 80.

19. Labour Party Research Department, *Handbook*, 1951, London, p. 299.

20. Mark Benney and Phyllis Geiss, "Social Class and Politics in Greenwich," *The British Journal of Sociology*, Vol. 1, No. 4 (Dec., 1950), pp. 310-27.

21. Euan Cooper-Willis, *Towards Equality* (London: Fabian Publications, Ltd., 1950), p. 6.

22. Max Weber, in H. H. Gerth and C. Wright Mills, trans. and eds., *From Max Weber* (London: Kegan Paul, Trench, Trubner and Co., Ltd., 1947), p. 93.

23. *Ibid.*, p. 228.

24. *Ibid.*, p. 213.

25. *Ibid.*, p. 215.

26. *Ibid.*, p. 224.

27. G. D. H. Cole, "Shall Socialism Fail?" I, The Democrat's Dilemma, *The New Statesman and Nation*, XLI, No. 1052 (May 5, 1951), p. 497.

28. Joseph A. Schumpeter, *Imperialism and Social Classes*, tr. by Heinz Norden (Oxford: Basil Blackwell, 1951), p. 214.

29. *Ibid.*, p. 198.

30. Max Weber, *op. cit.*, pp. 228-30.

31. George Simpson, "Class Analysis: What Class Is Not," *ASR*, IV, 827.

32. Harold W. Pfautz, "The Current Literature on Social Stratification: Critique and Bibliography," *AJS*, LVIII, 406.

33. Seymour M. Lipset and Reinhard Bendix, "Ideological Equalitarianism and Social Mobility in the United States," *Transactions of the Second World Congress of Sociology*, II, 35, 1954.

34. Gideon Sjoberg, "Are Social Classes in America Becoming More Rigid?" *ASR*, XVI, 775-83.

35. These men, of course, recognized the existence of differences in role and status in the population, but observed no system of statuses, status groups, or estates, which were comparable to the European situation at the respective times of writing.

Alexis de Toqueville, *Democracy in America*, 1835 and 1838, Phillips Bradley, ed. (New York: Alfred A. Knopf Co., 1945), Vols. I and II: "Among the novel objects that attracted my attention during my stay in the United States, nothing struck me more forcibly than the general equality among the people . . . it has no less effect on civil society than on government" (I, 3); and "In the United States, the citizens have no sort of pre-eminence over one another: they owe each other no mutual obedience or respect . . ." (II, 215). When speaking of informal associations or groupings, he says they are due to "accidental similarity of opinions and tastes . . . artificial and arbitrary distinctions" (II, 216). De Toqueville saw, however, the possibility in the future of the growth of an aristocracy of the manufacturers. (II, 158-61).

James Bryce, *The American Comonwealth* (London: MacMillan Co., 1891), Vol. II: "Classes are in America by no means the same thing as in the greater nations of Europe. . . . Their specific characters . . . are less marked even in typical individuals than would be the case in Europe, and are in many individuals scarcely recognizable" (p. 283). Bryce formulates seven occupational classes and discusses their influence on public opinion.

Harold J. Laski, *The American Democracy* (New York: The Viking Press, 1948): "For the ordinary American citizen no trace has remained of that feudal heritage which still has deep influence on the social relationships of most European countries. There is an equality between citizen and citizen. . . . There is no such habit of deference in the American workman . . . as in the English. *He is aware of an economic distinction of class between himself and his employer.* But he does not easily regard that economic distinction as entailing a social consequence . . ." (pp. 24-25. Italics mine). Laski saw the business class as a power group in the United States, and labor as a potential power group of political significance.

36. Robert E. L. Faris, "The Alleged Class System in the United States," *Proceedings of the Pacific Sociological Society, 1954,* published as Vol. XXII, No. 2, of the Research Studies of the State College of Washington (June, 1954).

37. Kurt Mayer, "The Theory of Social Classes," *Harvard Educational Review,* XXIII, 149-67.

38. "Class, Status, and Power in England," *supra.*

39. Florian Znaniecki, "Basic Problems of Contemporary Sociology," ASR, XIX, 519-24.

40. Lipset and Bendix, *op. cit.,* pp. 47-48.

41. R. H. Gretton, *The English Middle Class* (London: G. Bell and Sons, Ltd., 1919), pp. 1-10.

42. C. Wright Mills, *White Collar* (New York: Oxford University Press, 1951).

43. Morris Ginsberg, *Sociology* (London: Oxford University Press, 1934), p. 163.

Notes to Part III

1. For the conceptions of some English writers, see: A. M. Carr-Saunders and D. Caradog Jones, *A Survey of the Social Structure of England and Wales,* Second Edition (Oxford: Clarendon Press, 1937), pp. 66-67; R. H. Tawney, *Equality* (London: George Allen and Unwin, Ltd., 1931), p. 80; G. D. H. Cole, "The Conception of the Middle Class," *British Journal of Sociology,* Vol. I, No. 4 (Dec., 1950), p. 287; Morris Ginsberg, *Sociology* (London: Oxford University Press, 1934), p. 170; and Roy Lewis and Angus Maude, *The English Middle Classes* (London: Phoenix House, 1949), p. 17.

2. See "Class, Status and Power in England" *supra;* Joel B. Montague, Jr., "Research Related to Social Class in England," *ASR,* Vol. XVII, No. 2 (April, 1952), pp. 192-96; and "Bureaucracy and British Socialism," *infra.*

3. See Mark Abrams, *Social Surveys and Social Action* (London: Heineman, 1951), and D. L. Hobman, *The Welfare State* (London: John Murray, 1953).

4. T. Brennan, "The Working Class in the British Social Structure," *Transactions of the Third World Congress of Sociology,* III, 106. Also see G. D. H. Cole and Raymond Postgate, *The Common People* (London: Methuen, 1946).

5. *Ibid.,* p. 145.

6. *Annual Abstract of Statistics,* No. 93 (London: HMS, 1956), Table 267; *Handbook of Facts and Figures for Socialists* (London: Labour Party, 1951), p. 174.

7. G. D. H. Cole, "Is This Socialism?", *New Statesman Pamphlet,* 1954.

8. G. D. H. Cole, *Studies in Class Structure* (London: Routledge and Kegan Paul, 1955), p. 77.

9. Robert Bierstedt, "An Analysis of Social Power," *ASR,* Vol. XV, No. 6 (Dec., 1950), pp. 730-38.

10. See W. E. Styler, "Manual Workers and the Workers' Educational Association," *British Journal of Sociology,* Vol. IV, No. 1 (March, 1953), pp. 79-83.

11. Brennan, *op. cit.,* p. 109.

12. Richard Hoggart, *The Uses of Literacy* (London: Chatto and Winders, 1957).

13. See Melvin H. Tumin, "Some Unapplauded Consequences of Social Mobility," *Social Forces,* Vol. XXXVI, No. 1 (Oct., 1957), pp. 32-37.

14. *Ibid.,* p. 35.

15. Hoggart, *op. cit.,* p. 141ff.

16. *Ibid.,* p. 15.

17. There is much criticism of the new (1944) tripartite secondary schools and the selection procedure, but overall selection has roughly followed the distribution of intelligence as measured by I.Q. tests. See Joel B. Montague, Jr., "The New English Secondary Schools," *The Clearing House*, Vol. XXVI, No. 3 (Nov., 1951), pp. 131-35; Joel B. Montague, Jr., "The 'Eleven-Plus' Battle in Education in England," *The Clearing House*, Vol. XXXII, No. 5 (Jan., 1958), pp. 259-62; and Joel B. Montague, Jr., "Are Eton and Rugby Doomed by Socialism?", *The Clearing House*, Vol. XXXII, No. 6 (Feb., 1958), pp. 333-36.

18. G. D. H. Cole, *op. cit.*, p. 85. The following discussion draws upon this source.

19. *Ibid.*, pp. 70 and 97.

20. Roy Lewis and Angus Maude, *The English Middle Classes* (London: Phoenix House, 1949), p. 17. Public opinion polls have elicited responses which would place a somewhat higher percentage in the middle classes.

21. *Ibid.*

22. Cole, *op. cit.*, pp. 94-95.

23. Lewis and Maude, *op. cit.*

24. Cole, *op. cit.*

25. Lewis and Maude, *op. cit.*, p. viii.

26. *Ibid.*, p. vii.

27. *Ibid.*, pp. 277-301.

28. *Ibid.*, pp. 302-17.

29. *Ibid.*, p. 334.

30. *Ibid.*, p. 360.

31. *Ibid.*, pp. 359-60.

32. Cole, *op. cit.*, p. 96.

33. *Ibid.*, p. 70.

34. *Ibid.*, pp. 72-73.

35. *Ibid.*, pp. 65-66.

36. *Ibid.*, p. 67.

37. *Ibid.*, p. 129.

38. *Ibid.*, p. 73.

39. *Ibid.*, pp. 98 and 77.

40. *Ibid.*, p. 99.

41. *Ibid.*, p. 100.

42. These characteristics are not strictly unique to the professions. See Edward Gross, *Work and Society* (New York: Thomas Crowell, 1958), pp. 77-82.

43. A. M. Carr-Saunders and P. A. Wilson, *The Professions* (London: Oxford, at the Clarendon Press, 1933), p. 491.

44. See T. H. Marshall, *Citizenship and Social Class* (Cambridge: Cambridge University Press, 1950), pp. 132-35.

45. Gross, *op. cit.*, p. 79.

46. Carr-Saunders and Wilson, *op. cit.*, p. 485.

47. *Social Services in Britain* (London: Central Office of Information, Pamphlet No. 3, HM Stationery Office), 1956, p. 23 (emphasis mine).

48. Roy Lewis and Angus Maude, *Professional People* (London: Phoenix House, 1953), p. 178.

49. For a description of the National Health Service, see *Health Services in Britain* (London: Central Office of Information reference Pamphlet No. 20, HM Stationery Office, 1962); M. Penelope Hall, *The Social Services of Modern England* (London: Routledge and Kegan Paul, 1952); R. M. Titmuss, essays on 'The Welfare State' (London: George Allen and Unwin), 1958, and "Socialized Medicine," *infra*.

50. Lewis and Maude, *op. cit.*, p. 175.

51. See "Socialized Medicine," *infra*.

52. *Health Services in Britain*, *op. cit.*, pp. 13-14.

53. *Britain, An Official Handbook* (London: HM Stationery Office, 1956), p. 273.

54. *Ibid.*, pp. 272-73; also see Lewis and Maude, *op. cit.*, pp. 231-57, for comparisons with other professions.

55. Marshall, *op. cit.*, p. 142.

56. *Ibid.*, p. 145.

57. See John Moore, *Portrait of Elmbury, the Biography of a Market Town* (London, 1945), pp. 16-18.

58. *Tewkesbury—Draft Analysis,* Gloucestershire Town and Country Planning Authority (mimeographed), 1957, pp. 3-5.

59. *Ibid.*, p. 9; the working force included a number of non-resident military personnel.

60. See "Social Class Status of the Small Farm Freeholder in the English Midlands," *infra*.

61. See W. P. Baker, *The English Village* (London, 1953).

62. See D. V. Glass, *Social Mobility in Britain* (Glencoe, 1954), and "Some Aspects of Class, Status and Power Relations in England," *supra*.

63. See Richard Hoggart, *The Uses of Literacy* (London, 1957).

64. *Ibid.*; G. D. H. Cole, *op. cit.*; T. Brennan, *op. cit.*, pp. 106-12. Also see Joel B. Montague, Jr., "Research Related to Social Class in England," *ASR*, XVII (April, 1952), 192-96.

65. See T. H. Pear, *English Social Differences* (London: Allen and Unwin, 1955), pp. 85-118.

66. See "Changes in Class and Status of Occupational Groups in an English Town," *supra*.

67. Max Weber, in H. H. Gerth and C. Wright Mills, *From Max*

Weber (London: Kegan Paul, Trench, Trubner and Company, Ltd., 1947), pp. 196-224.

68. *Ibid.*

69. Hyneman apparently does this when he says, "Men and women brought together to work in large organizations constitute bureaucracy." Charles S. Hyneman, *Bureaucracy in a Democracy* (New York: Harper and Brothers, 1950), p. 3. Actually, only those who occupy offices whose function is control should be designated as bureaucrats.

70. See J. Donald Kingsley, *Representative Bureaucracy* (Yellow Springs: The Antioch Press, 1944).

71. K. C. Wheare, "Bureaucracy in a Democracy," a review of *Bureaucracy in a Democracy*, by Charles S. Hyneman, in *Public Administration*, Institute of Public Administration, London: 29:146-47, Summer, 1951.

72. Wheare, *ibid.*, p. 147.

73. Hyneman, *op. cit.*, p. 7.

74. Kingsley, *op. cit.*, pp. 287-88.

75. See L. White, C. Bland, W. Sharp, and M. Marx, *Civil Service Abroad* (New York: McGraw-Hill, 1935), pp. 44-52.

76. "Some Aspects of Class, Status and Power Relations in England," *supra.*

77. S. M. Lipset, "Bureaucracy and Social Reform," *Research Studies of the State College of Washington*, 17:11-17, (March, 1949).

78. This is more true of the National Coal Board than it is of the others. In fact, the boards controlling gas, iron and steel, and the National Health Service are rather extensively decentralized.

79. D. G. MacRae, "Domestic Record of the Labour Government," *Political Quarterly*, London: 20:1-11 (January-March, 1949).

80. Macrae, *op. cit.*, pp. 4-5.

81. See W. H. Morris Jones, *Socialism and Bureaucracy* (London: Fabian Publications, Ltd., 1949).

82. W. H. Morris Jones, *ibid.*, p. 12.

83. D. L. Hobman, *The Welfare State* (London, John Murray, 1953), p. 1.

84. *Health Services in Britain*, Central Office of Information, reference pamphlet No. 20, H.M.S.O., London, 1962, p. 7.

85. *Ibid.*

86. *Ibid.*, p. 8.

87. *Handbook for General Medical Practitioners*, Ministry of Health, H.M.S.O. London, 1955, pp. 1-2. Members of Councils receive no salary; recently they have been allowed remuneration for limited expenses.

88. *Report of the Ministry of Health for the Year Ended 31st*

December, 1961, Part I, The Health and Welfare Services, H.M.S.O., London, 1962, p. 44.

89. *Health Services in Britain, op. cit.*, pp. 13-15.

90. *Ibid.*

91. *Ibid.*

92. See *The British Medical Journal* (April 6, 1957), which is the source of much of the following discussion.

93. *Payment of Doctors in the National Health Service*, British Information Ser-ID 1138, February, 1961, New York.

94. Reference is to working papers of a study by Joel B. Montague, Jr. and Bhopinder S. Bolaria concerned with professionalism in medicine in the National Health Service and in the U.S. which was carried out in 1962. Data were collected by interviews with approximately 150 doctors in selected areas of England and a like number in the U.S.

95. See Almont Lindsey, *Socialized Medicine in England and Wales*, (Chapel Hill: University of North Carolina Press, 1962), reference taken from abstract "How Socialized Medicine Works," *The New Republic* (June 4, 1962), p. 11.

96. *Socialization of the Professions, supra.*

97. *New Statesman* (January 26, 1962).

98. Working papers, *op. cit.*

99. *Ibid.*

100. *Ibid.*

101. *British Medical Journal*, Editorial (December 2, 1950).

102. The complete study was published as a book. See B. Able-Smith and R. M. Titmuss, *The Cost of the National Health Service in England and Wales* (Cambridge: Cambridge University Press, 1956).

103. R. M. Titmuss, *Essays on the 'Welfare State'* (London: George Allen and Unwin, Ltd., 1958), p. 148.

104. *Ibid.*, p. 149, including data for years since the original study was made.

105. Lindsey, *op. cit.*

106. Titmuss, *op. cit.*, pp. 150-51.

107. *British Medical Journal*, Editorial (July 14, 1962).

108. Jean Floud and A. H. Halsey, "The Sociology of Education," *Current Sociology*, Vol. VII, No. 3 (1958), pp. 165-93.

109. *Ibid.*, pp. 177-78.

110. "Class, Status and Power in England," *supra*. Also see Joel B. Montague, Jr., "Research Related to Social Class in England," *op. cit.*, Vol. XVII, No. 2 (April, 1952), pp. 192-96.

111. O. C. Cox, *Caste, Class and Race* (Garden City, New York: Doubleday, 1948).

112. R. H. Tawney, *Equality* (London: George Allen and Unwin Co., Ltd., 1952 printing).

113. Bagehot, *The English Constitution* (1867), pp. 50-54.

114. N. Hans, *Comparative Education* (London, 1949), p. 133, as quoted by D. V. Glass, *op. cit.*, pp. 27-28.

115. E. Thring, *Education and School* (1864), pp. 4 and 5, as quoted by Tawney, *op. cit.*, p. 19.

116. Frederic Engels, *The Condition of the Working Class in England in 1844* (London: Allen and Unwin, Ltd., 1950 printing), p. 278.

117. *Education in Britain*, Central Office of Information, reference pamphlet No. 7 (London: H.M. Stationery Office, 1956).

118. A. F. Wells, *The Local Social Survey in Great Britain* (London: Allen and Unwin, 1935), p. 13.

119. D. Caradog Jones, *Social Surveys* (London: Hutchinson's University Library), p. 9.

120. D. V. Glass, *op. cit.*

121. *Ibid.*, pp. 188 and 222.

122. J. L. Gray and P. Moshinsky, "Ability and Opportunity in English Education," pp. 334-77 in L. Hogben (ed.), *Political Arithmetic* (London: Allen and Unwin, 1938).

123. Jean E. Floud, A. H. Halsey and R. M. Martin, *Social Class and Educational Opportunity* (London: Heinemann, 1957).

124. *Ibid.*

125. D. L. Hobman, *op. cit.*

126. Glass, *op. cit.*, p. 27.

127. *Educational Reconstruction*, Cmd., 6458, 1943, p. 3, as referred to in Glass, *ibid.*, p. 23.

128. Butler, as quoted by Glass, *op. cit.*, p. 27.

129. *15 to 18*, Report of the Central Advisory Council for Education—England, Vol. I, Ministry of Education (London: H.M. Stationery Office), p. 55.

130. *The Nation's Schools* (Ministry of Education), 1945, as quoted in Michael Young, *The Rise of Meritocracy, 1870-2033* (New York: Random House, 1959), p. 7.

131. *Education in Britain, op. cit.*, p. 8.

132. J. D. Scott, *Life in Britain* (London: Eyre and Spottiswoode, 1956), pp. 165-66.

133. *15 to 18, op. cit.*, p. 203.

134. *Challenge to Britain* (Labour Party publication, 1953).

135. *Times Educational Supplement* (May 17, 1957).

136. Glass, *op. cit.*, pp. 25-26.

137. Michael Young and Peter Willmott, *Family and Kinship in East London* (Glencoe: The Free Press, 1957), p. 14.

138. A. H. Halsey, "Genetics, Social Structure and Intelligence," *British Journal of Sociology*, Vol. IX, No. 1 (March, 1958), p. 27. Also see H. T. Himmelweit and J. Whitfield, "Mean Intelligence Test Scores of a Random Sample of Occupations," *British Industrial Medicine*, Vol. I, 1947; and A. H. Halsey and L. Gardner, "Selection for Secondary Education Achievement in Four Grammar Schools," *British Journal of Sociology*, Vol. IV, No. 1 (March, 1953), pp. 60-75.

139. Floud and Halsey, "The Sociology of Education," *op. cit.*, p. 175.

140. Halsey and Gardner, *op. cit.*

141. Jean Floud and A. H. Halsey, "Intelligence Tests, Social Class and Selection for Secondary Schools," *British Journal of Sociology*, Vol. VIII, No. 1 (March, 1950); also see Joel B. Montague, Jr., "The New English Secondary Schools" *Clearing House*, Vol. XXVI, No. 3 (November, 1951); "The Eleven-Plus Battle in Education in England," *Clearing House*, Vol. XXXII, No. 5 (January, 1958) and "Some Problems of Selection for Secondary Schools in England—Implications for the U.S.," *Journal of Educational Sociology*, Vol. XXXII, No. 8 (April, 1959).

142. *15 to 18*, *op. cit.*, p. 22.

143. *Times Educational Supplement*, June 28, 1957.

144. *Ibid.*

145. *15 to 18*, *op. cit.*, p. 23.

146. Scott, *op. cit.*, p. 169.

147. Glass, *op. cit.*, pp. 22-23.

148. *The Observer*, June 9, 1957.

149. Norwood, quoted in Glass, *op. cit.*, p. 23.

150. *Education in Britain*, *op. cit.*

151. *The Public Schools*, Conservative Party publication (London, 1957), p. 18.

152. *Ibid.*, pp. 25-27.

153. *Challenge to Britain*, *op. cit.*

154. Glass, *op. cit.*, p. 23.

155. Young, *The Rise of Meritocracy*, *op. cit.*

Notes to Part IV

1. See A. B. Hollingshead, "Behavior Systems as a Field for Research," *ASR*, IV, 6 (Dec., 1939), pp. 816-22.

2. John Hall and D. Caradog Jones, "Social Grading of Occupations," *British Journal of Sociology*, I, 1 (March, 1950), pp. 31-55.

3. See Ronald Taft, "The Social Grading of Occupations in Australia," *British Journal of Sociology*, IV, 2 (June, 1953), pp. 181-88, and A. A. Congalton, "Social Grading of Occupations in New

Zealand" *British Journal of Sociology*, IV, 1 (March, 1953), pp. 45-59.

4. Hall and Jones, *op. cit.*, p. 51.

5. *Ibid.*, pp. 48-49.

6. U.S. Bureau of the Census, *Population: Comparative Occupational Statistics for the United States, 1870 to 1940* (Washington, D.C.: U.S. Government Printing Office, 1943), pp. 176-79.

7. *Dictionary of Occupational Titles* (Washington, D.C.: U.S. Government Printing Office).

8. Talcott Parsons, "A Revised Analytical Approach to the Theory of Social Stratification," in Reinhard Bendix and Seymour M. Lipset, eds., *Class, Status, and Power* (Glencoe, Ill.: The Free Press, 1953), pp. 92-128.

9. Harold W. Pfautz, "The Current Literature on Social Stratification: Critique and Bibliography," *AJS*, LVIII (January, 1953), 391-418.

10. Max Lerner, "The Idea of American Civilization," *Journal of Social Issues*, Vol. VII, No. 4 (1951), p. 31.

11. Margaret Mead, "National Character," in L. S. Kroeber (ed.), *Anthropology Today* (Chicago: University of Chicago Press, 1953), pp. 642-67; Gregory Bateson, "Morale and National Character," in Goodwin Watson (ed.), *Civilian Morale* (New York: Houghton Mifflin Co., 1942), pp. 71-91; and Geoffrey Gorer, "The Concept of National Character," *Science News*, No. 18 (Nov., 1950), pp. 105-22.

12. A. R. Lindesmith and A. L. Strauss, "A Critique of Culture-Personality Writings," *ASR*, XV (1950), 587-600.

13. Ralph Linton, "Problems of Status Personality," in S. Sargent and M. Smith (eds.), *Culture and Personality* (New York: Viking Fund, 1949), pp. 167 and 170.

14. J. H. Steward, comment in Tax, Eiseley, Rouse and Voegelin (eds.), *An Appraisal of Anthropology Today* (Chicago: University of Chicago Press, 1953), p. 140.

15. Richard Centers, "Children of the New Deal; Social Stratification and Adolescent Attitudes," *International Journal of Opinion and Attitude Research*, No. 4 (1950), pp. 315-35. It is assumed that the responses of these adolescents are meaningful in terms of the relevant culture of the respective regions.

16. "Comparative Prestige Ranking of Occupations in an American City with Reference to Hall's and Jones' Study," *supra;* and U.S. Bureau of the Census, *Population: Comparative Occupational Statistics for the United States, 1870-1940* (Washington: Government Printing Office, 1943), pp. 176-79.

17. Allison Davis and Robert J. Havighurst, "Social Class and Color Differences in Child-Rearing," *ASR*, XI (1946), 698-710; Herbert H. Hyman, "The Value System of Different Classes: A Social Psychological Contribution to the Analysis of Stratification,"

in Reinhard Bendix and Seymour Lipset, *op. cit.*; Bernice L. Neugarten, "Social Class and Friendship Among School Children," *AJS*, LI (1946), pp. 305-13; W. Lloyd Warner, Robert J. Havighurst and Martin B. Loeb, *Who Shall Be Educated?* (New York: Harper and Bros., 1944).

18. J. A. Jahn, "The Statistical-Experimental Evaluation of Qualitative and Quantitative Predictions" (unpublished paper prepared for presentation at the annual meeting of the American Sociological Society, September, 1953).

19. See Rollo May, *The Meaning of Anxiety* (New York: The Ronald Press, 1950), pp. 193-200; and Allison Davis and Robert Havighurst, *Father of the Man* (Boston: Houghton Mifflin Co., 1947), pp. 212-13.

20. Alex Inkeles and Daniel J. Levinson, "National Character, the Study of Modal Personality and Socio-cultural Systems," in G. Lindzey (ed.), *Handbook of Social Psychology* (Cambridge: Addison-Wesley Publishing Co., 1954), p. 983.

21. Hylan Lewis, *Blackways of Kent* (Chapel Hill: University of North Carolina Press, 1955), pp. 326-27.

INDEX

Abel-Smith, B., 143, 236n.
Abrams, Mark, 232n.
Accountant, comparative prestige of, 97, 170-77
Aggressiveness, English and American boys, 196ff.
American Medical Association, and the National Health Service, 144
Anxiety, and class, 208-13
Archenholtz, J. W., 49
Aristocracy, British, 66ff.
Artisans, 118
Attitudes, and class, 196ff.; mobility, 215ff.; prediction of, 201ff.
Authority, attitude toward, 196ff.

Baghot, W., 237n.
Baker, W. P., 234n.
Bankers, 118
Barber, Bernard, 226n.
Bartender, comparative prestige of, 170-77
Basic character, 55
Basic personality type, 55
Bateson, G., XIII, 61, 193, 228n., 229n., 239n.
Bendix, R., 26, 28, 79, 221n., 225n., 226n., 227n., 230n., 231n., 239n., 240n.
Benney, Mark, 230n.
Bentham, Jeremy, 48
Bevan, Aneurin, 133, 135
Beveridge Report, 132, 140, 149
Bierstedt, Robert, 90, 229n., 230n., 232n.
Bismarck, 48
Blackwell, J. E., 222n.
Bland, C., 235n.
Bolaria, Bhopinder S., 236n.
Booth, Charles, 88
Bottomore, T. B., 224n.
Bowley, A. L., 149
Brennan, T., 232n.

Bricklayers, comparative prestige of, 170-77
British Medical Association, 136ff.; as quoted on the AMA, 144
Bryce, James, 80, 231n.
Buckley, Walter, 225n., 226n.; on Davis and Moore, 35-36
Bureaucracy, 74, 75, 76; characteristics of, 125-26; and nationalization, 126; and socialism, 125-30
Business executives, 97; comparative prestige of, 170-77
Butler, R. A., 150, 160

Carpenters, comparative prestige of, 170-77
Carr, E. H., 50-51, 52, 227n., 228n.
Carr-Saunders, A. M., 68, 71, 105, 229n., 232n., 233n., 234n.
Centers, Richard, 224n., 239n.
Chartist movement, 70
Child training practices, 58, 62
Churchill, Winston, 132, 140
Civil servants, 97, 127; comparative prestige of, 170-77
Civil Service, British, 97, 127ff.
Class, and anxiety, 208ff.; and attitudes, 193ff.; concepts of, 19ff.; conflict, 23, 24, 70, 83, 90, 95, 99; confused with status, 20; and culture, XII; defined, 65; and education, 146ff.; and health care, 132ff.; names given, 184-85; as potential groups, 83; in U.S., 78ff.; see also working class, middle class, aristocracy
Clergymen, 117
Clerks, 118
Cole, G. D. H., 68, 72, 75, 97, 100, 101, 102, 103, 104, 160, 229n., 230n., 232n., 233n., 234n.
Colquhoun, Patrick, 89